First Impressions

First Impressions

PROGRAMME DIRECTOR: JIM SWEETMAN

CollinsEducational
An imprint of HarperCollins*Publishers*

ISBN 0 00 323014 7

First published 1989 by Collins Educational,
8 Grafton Street, London W1X 3LA.

Reprinted 1990,1992

Cover and book designed by Christie Archer Design, London.

Cover illustration by Simon Fell.

Typeset by Rowland Phototypesetting Limited,
Bury St Edmunds, Suffolk.

Printed and bound in Hong Kong.

Contents

SCHOOL PASSPORT

When you leave the country you have to take your passport with you. It tells people in other countries who you are and where you have come from. In this unit you are going to prepare your own school passport. This will tell other people in your class – and in other classes – quite a lot about you.

you will be....

Relating personal experience

Presenting information

Following instructions

Filling in your description page

To get a passport, you normally have to fill in an application form, giving information about yourself. An official then sends you back your passport with the description page filled in, ready for you to sign.

Because this is a school passport, you don't have to apply. You are also trusted to fill in the description page yourself. Your teacher will give you a blank form.

Before you start, read the notes on the right very carefully. Also, look at the completed page opposite so that you can see what *your* completed page should look like.

NOTES

Use these notes to help you fill in the **description** page of your passport.

1 Write your **surname** (your last name) in capital letters. The rest you may write in your normal handwriting.

2 Remember to include all your **first names**.

3 Write how long you have lived at your present **home address** in years – and months if you know this.

4 Your **place of birth** – You need to put the town and country.

5 Write your **date of birth** and **age** in numbers.

6 You can guess your **height** and **weight** if you don't know them.

7 You may not have any **distinguishing features**. If not, leave this blank.

8 The completed description must be **checked** by a friend and **signed** by your English teacher, who is the School Passport Officer.

DESCRIPTION

Surname Hope

First name(s) Lisa Karen

Home address 7 Old Oak Lane
Winchester Hampshire

Post Code SP14 9NG

How long have you lived there? 3 years, 6 months

Place of birth St Mary's Ward, King's Hospital
Camberwell, London

Date of birth 8/11/77 Age 11

Weight 43 kg

Height 1.60 metres

Colour of hair Black

Colour of eyes Brown

Distinguishing features Small mole on chin

Description checked by Jill Wilson

Usual signature Lisa K. Hope

Signed G S Newton School Passport Officer

Date of issue 14 3 89

THIS PASSPORT IS VALID FOR 5 YEARS AND RENEWABLE FOR A FURTHER 2 YEARS.

Designing your visa pages

To make your visa pages, you will need to fold sheets of A4 paper in two.

1. Make a list of the places you have visited so far in your life. The list can include such places as your grandparents' house, a museum or a sports ground as well as holiday spots and other countries. The list can be as long and as varied as you like.

2. From this list of places, choose about six that you especially want to remember.

3. For each chosen place, design a passport stamp or 'visa'. Each stamp must have the place name in clear lettering. It must also have a design, so that it all looks rather like a badge.

- Make a rough sketch of each stamp design before putting the final copy on your passport page.
- Think about how a passport visa page looks. See how the stamps overlap each other. Try this on your own pages to make them look realistic.

Designing your passport cover

To make your cover, you will need to fold one sheet of A4 paper or card in two. Here are some ideas for what you could then include on your cover:

FRONT COVER OUTSIDE

Look at a real passport cover. Your cover needs your name, the school's name, a made-up passport number and a design. The design could be a copy of your school's coat of arms or a new school badge designed by you.

FRONT COVER INSIDE

Paste in a small photo of yourself if you can get one, or draw a sketch of your head and shoulders.

BACK COVER INSIDE

Write down, in alphabetical order, all the places on your original list of places visited that you did *not* design a stamp for.

BACK COVER OUTSIDE

Write here (again in alphabetical order) all the places you hope to visit in your lifetime. Think BIG – the South Pole, the Moon, for example. Don't just put the name of a country, e.g. America. Put the name of actual places, e.g.:

The Grand Canyon, America
The Great Barrier Reef, Australia
The River Nile, Egypt.

Use an atlas to help you.

Making use of your school passport

Once you've finished your passport, you can make use of it in lots of different ways.

- Get together with a partner – perhaps someone in your class or another class whom you don't know very well. Swap passports. Then chat together about your past – and your hopes for the future.
- Show your passport to grown ups. Ask them to show you their passports and tell you about the places they have visited.
- Up-date your passport as you go through the year. Add to the list of places visited and design more visas for them. You could also change the entries for your height and weight, if necessary.

Tips for Success

- Make sure all the information is accurate. Check that the names of towns and countries are spelt correctly.
- Take care with your handwriting. Use capital letters to make the most important information stand out.
- Think carefully before deciding on your list of places visited.
- Design your passport pages as neatly as possible. Make rough versions of your visa designs first.

LETTER TO THE FUTURE

In this unit you are going to write a letter to someone you will never meet but who is quite likely to exist! You will be writing a letter to your great-grandchild to be opened when he or she reaches fifteen.

you will be....

- Sharing ideas
- Reporting on discussion
- Describing imaginatively

Thinking about your reader

You are not writing this letter to someone you know. Before you begin to write it, you'll need to think very hard about what your great-grandchild is likely to want to read about. You will need to decide what ingredients will make the letter interesting.

Soldiers departing from Waterloo station during the First World War, 1914–1918.

Beach scene, 1913. Are you surprised by the clothes?

A formal family group, 1910. One of the women is probably the children's nanny or governess.

STAGE ONE . . . *THINKING BACKWARDS*

1. Get into small groups. Discuss what you would like to read about in a letter from your great-grandparents written by them when they were your age. They'd have been writing sometime between 1910 and 1920. The photographs and captions on this page may give you some starting points for your discussion. Each of you should make a list of possible headings such as : clothes, food, friends, sport, important people and events.

2. Now share your ideas with another group. One person from your group should move to another group and give them an idea of what you were talking about. Someone from another group will also share their ideas with you. Are they the same as yours? Are there extra headings to note down on your list?

3. You will now have a set of headings around which you can develop your own letter. You will probably only select those items which interest you most, rather than attempting to cover all of them.

Busy London traffic, 1912. The trams in this picture are motorised but other vans and carts are still horse-drawn. Can you spot the car?

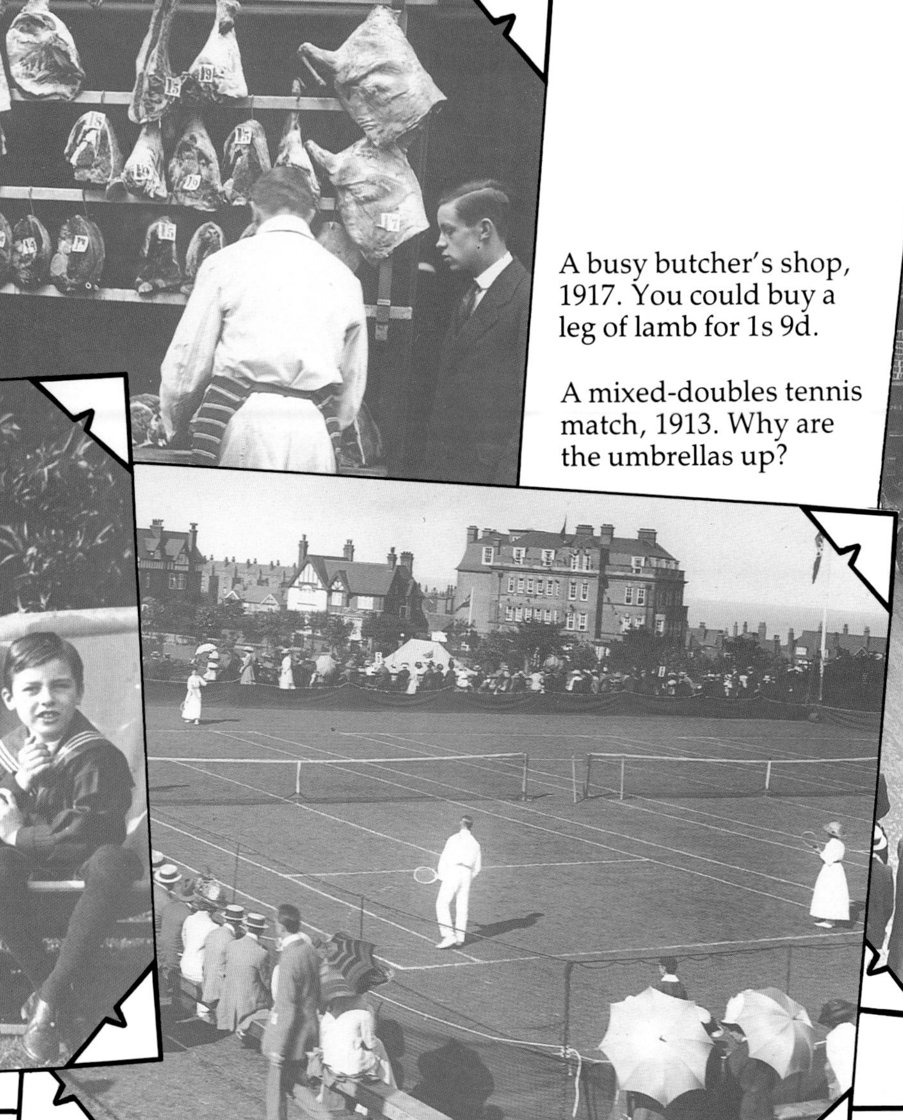

A busy butcher's shop, 1917. You could buy a leg of lamb for 1s 9d.

A mixed-doubles tennis match, 1913. Why are the umbrellas up?

STAGE TWO . . . *THINKING FORWARD*

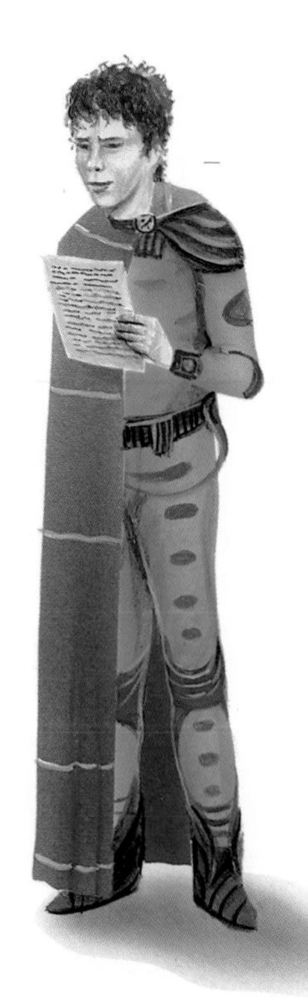

4 Before you begin the letter you need to think a little further about your reader and the world he or she will be living in.

On your own, spend some time jotting down your ideas about what life may be like in eighty years or so. You could think about some of these points to begin with:

- Will people still be living in houses or flats with a roof, windows and a front door or . . .?
- Will they be driving cars or . . .?
- Will they be wearing leather, wool and cotton or . . .?
- Will they be eating meat and vegetables or . . .?
- Will they be reading books and writing with pens or . . .?

5 Think about these questions too:

- Are there words and phrases which you use now, which a reader might find difficult to understand in eighty years time?
- What sorts of things will need explaining carefully to your great-grandchild?

These letters may give you some idea of the problems.

25 Hampton Villas
15th March

Dear Great-Grandson,
There's a load to tell you. We have lots of gadgets at home including a CD player and a microwave. Do you still have them? Our car is an Austin Maestro. We also have an au pair called Karin and a Doberman called Eric. I wonder if you keep pets now?
School is yuk but Liverpool are fantastic. I expect they're still top. Are any of the players robots now?

School
Friday Afternoon

Dear Great Granddaughter,
It's well wicked in the 1980s. We have walkmans and number twos on our heads and we're crazy about Bros and Rick Astley. f you were here you could see 'Neighbours'. s great. Then there's 'Dynasty'. I expect at's still being repeated in case missed any of it!!

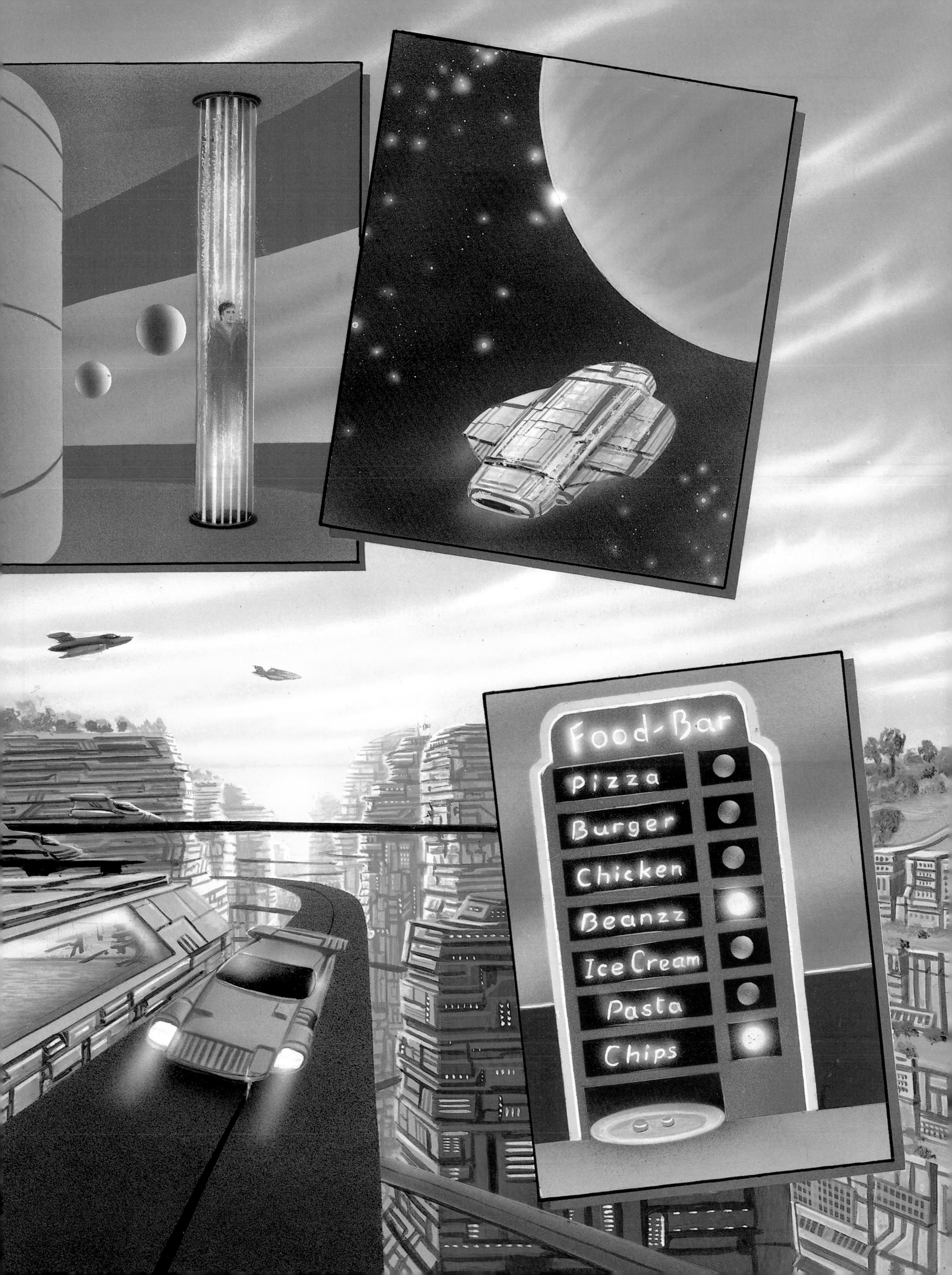
Food-Bar
Pizza
Burger
Chicken
Beanzz
Ice Cream
Pasta
Chips

STAGE THREE . . . *DRAFTING YOUR LETTER*

6 You are writing to a relation whom you've never met. Will your letter be friendly and chatty? Will it be quite formal? Jot down some possible beginnings and endings to the letter.

7 Look back at the list of ingredients you wrote down. Decide which you are going to write about and produce an *outline* for your letter.

Remember that the outline must include:

- **An opening paragraph**

  Experiment with this until it says what you want it to say. It needs to grab your reader's attention.

- **A sequence of paragraph headings**

  These should show the way in which your ideas are going to develop.

- **A final paragraph**

  This needs to form a strong ending to your letter. It might leave your reader with an interesting idea or question to think about.

8 Now write the first draft of your letter. Use a double page of your book and write only on the left-hand page, leaving the other side free for comments and revisions. Make sure that you put your address and the date in full at the top right-hand corner of your letter.

9 Read through your draft carefully. Then write down on the right-hand page any comments and notes for revisions. Also write down any questions you want to ask a partner, or your teacher, about the way your draft is written.

Now, get together with a partner. They must help you by putting themselves in the shoes of your great-grandchild. They must tell you if there are words, sentences or ideas which they can't understand.

10 Produce your final draft. Check it for mistakes. Then copy it out (or type it) ready for sealing in an envelope. You may wish to keep a spare copy to remember what you've said. Write instructions on the envelope about when, and by whom, the letter is to be opened. You could make your letter part of a *time-capsule*. This is a sealed container which is stored in a safe place, sometimes even in the foundations of a new building. If your letter was to be put in a time-capsule what else would you put in? Wherever you place your letter, don't forget about it. And maybe, in eighty years time, your great-grandchild *will* read it.

Tips for Success

- Think and plan carefully before you start to write. Don't rush any of the ten steps.
- Set your letter out neatly.
- Listen to the comments your partner makes and be willing to change what you have written.
- Think of your great-grandchild as a friend and write to him or her in that way.

GAZ
April 3rd 1989
NOT TO BE
OPENED UNTIL
2070

Bags of Character

The clothes people wear can say a lot about their personalities. So can the bags they carry. This unit looks at bags and the stories they can tell.

you will be....

- Sharing ideas
- Presenting information
- Reporting on discussion
- Writing a story

Starting on the outside

Look at the bags on this page. Do they suggest anything about their owners?

For each bag, jot down your thoughts about what the owner may be like. You might want to organise your thoughts under the headings below. These are only starting points. You may want to add to them.

Age Child? Teenager? Middle-aged? Elderly?

Sex Male? Female?

Occupation Office job? Outdoor Job? Works in a town?

Hobbies Sport? Music? Walking?

Physical appearance Tall? Short? Tidy? Untidy? Smartly dressed? Casually dressed?

Personality Jolly? Shy? Likes to stand out from the crowd?

Now join with a partner and compare your descriptions. Are they similar? What are the main differences?

You could now look at the bags used by people in your class. Does their appearance tell you anything about their owners?

BAG F

BAG E

BAG B

BAG C

BAG D

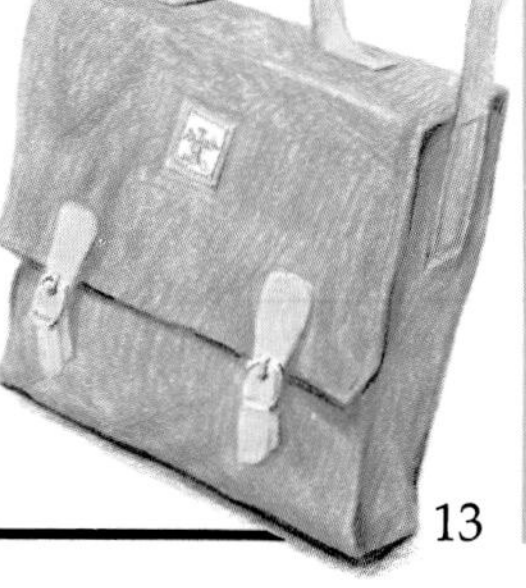

Looking inside

Divide into groups of four. Imagine that your group is a team of detectives investigating the theft of secret documents from an office at the Ministry of Defence. The thief was disturbed and dropped his holdall but he escaped with Top Secret documents.

THE ONLY CLUE IS THE BAG!

Your group task is to discover as much about the thief as you can by looking hard at the objects in the bag. Before you start, appoint a secretary to note down what you say.

FIRST . . .

Each person must choose an object, look at it carefully and describe it in detail to the rest of the group. What does it tell you about the thief? Look for clues about his physical appearance, habits, movements, nationality or whatever.
Do this until all the objects have been described.

THEN . . .

You now have to work the secretary's notes up into a formal report. The report must state any conclusions you have come to. Your teacher can provide you with a report form to fill in or you can design your own.

AND PRESENT YOUR REPORT . . .

One of the group must give your report to the class. When each group has reported back, you will have time to add other groups' suggestions to your final written report. You can complete this final report either in your groups or individually.

Tips for Success

- Use your imagination when looking at the objects. You are trying to build up as detailed a picture of the thief as possible.
- If you're the secretary, note down the main suggestions and ideas – not everything that is said.
- Argue as much as you like, but then agree on one report.
- If you're reporting back to the class, be clear and concise.
- Your final written report should be neat, clear and as full as possible.

Designer bags

As a group or individually, make up your own bag. You can do this on paper or you can make it more exciting by bringing in real objects from home. The rest of the group – or the rest of the class – have to guess whom the bag belongs to. Try designing the bags of famous people – or teachers!

LOST PROPERTY

Here are the contents of two bags that were found at the side of a busy road. Choose ONE of them and decide what sort of person owned the bag and where they might have been. Write a story which explains how the bag came to be there and why it contains some of the things it does.

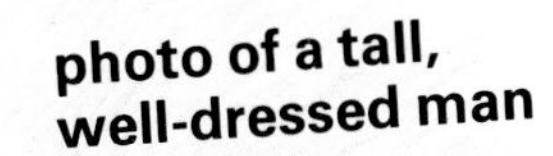

- **photo of a tall, well-dressed man**
- **envelope with an Edinburgh postmark**
- **leather desk diary**
- **crumpled handkerchief**
- **holiday brochure**
- **alarm clock**
- **copy of the *Financial Times***
- **paperback romance**
- **bank statement showing £5000 recently withdrawn**

- **padlock**
- **Pan-Am luggage ticket showing New York–Athens–London flight**
- **pack of cigars**
- **blonde wig**
- **lipstick**
- **large piece of soft cloth (slightly oily in places)**
- **map of London Underground with Westminster ringed in red ink**
- **copy of the Evening Standard**

LIST POEMS

This unit shows you how to make poems out of the simplest things. You will learn to build poems from 'lists'. You will discover that many poets also use lists to turn their thoughts and ideas into poems.

you will be....

- Giving an opinion
- Writing a poem
- Describing imaginatively
- Responding to a writer

LIKES AND DISLIKES

You are going to make a list of things you like and dislike, and then build a poem from it. But first, to give you some ideas, look at the poems below. They were both written by first years, and both started life as a list of likes and dislikes.

I like Neighbours, but loathe Crossroads,
I like frogs but can't stand toads.
I love my mum, but hate her moans,
I like fish'n'chips but can't stand the bones.
I think Bros are gorgeous but loathe Tom Jones,
I enjoy listening to people but not to their groans.

I like best butter but don't like stork,
I like roast beef, but don't like pork.
I like Coca-Cola but don't like tea
The thing I like best is just being me.

Gillian Newham

I like hot days
beans and sausages
I like a cat sleeping on my lap
and the smell of grass.

I like winning at Monopoly
Chinese food
kissing my pet frog

I like choosing my own clothes
I like a good laugh
I like the dark.

Form 1B/E Bedwas Comprehensive School

Join with a partner and talk about the poems. These questions may help you:

— Which poem is easier to read aloud?

— In the rhyming poem, do the rhymes sound natural? Do you think some of the words have been chosen *because* they rhyme and not for any other reason?

— Which poem do you think looks better on the page?

— Which poem uses the most unusual ideas? Can you think of a reason for this?

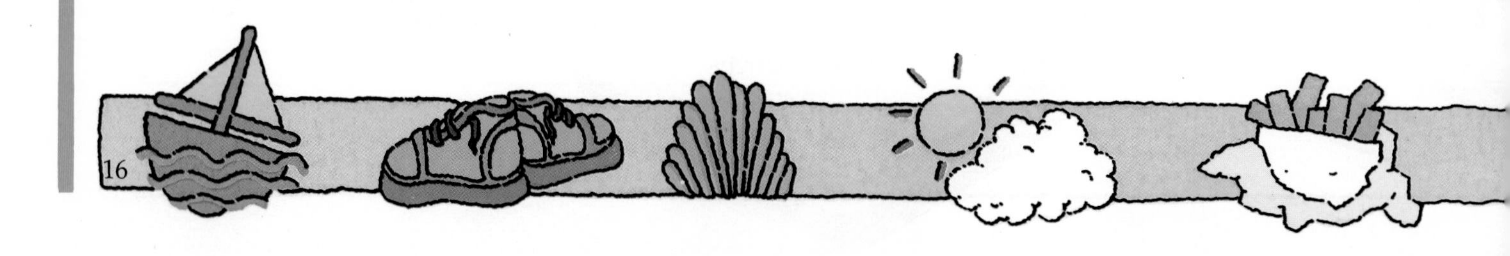

Now, it is your turn . . .

1 Take a blank sheet of paper. Write down two headings, LIKES and DISLIKES. Then give yourself five minutes or so to note down all the likes and dislikes that come into your head. Put *all* your ideas down. They don't have to be in any particular order. They don't have to be in sentences either.

This sort of activity is sometimes called 'brainstorming'. It is a good way of starting to think about a new idea, or about different answers to a problem.

2 Once you have your list, discuss it with a partner and see if you want to add to it before you write your poem.

3 Making your list into a poem isn't just a matter of writing it out. You will have to decide how to edit and order it. Editing means deciding what you want to take out, add, or change. You may want to add more detail to some of the things you wrote down.

For example, if you wrote down that you like apples, which ones do you like best? Green ones? Crisp ones? Sweet ones?

You may also decide you only want to use some of the things in *one* of your lists.

Ordering is also important. What are you going to put at the beginning of your poem? What are you going to end with? Are you going to mix up your likes and dislikes? If you're going to use rhyme, this may decide the order you put things in.

4 Finally, you need to think about who is going to be reading your poem.

— Is it just for yourself – a private poem?
— Will it be read by your friends, your teacher or the class?
— Is this a poem you would like your parents to see?
— Could it be published in a class newspaper or a school magazine?

If you are writing the poem purely for yourself, you may feel happy making it very personal – you may give away some of your innermost feelings about things. If you decide you're writing it to be read by others, you may decide you'd rather make it more distant and humorous.

Tips for Success

- Edit and order your lists. You don't have to use all the things you wrote down.
- Think about the shape of your poem.
- If you use rhyme, be careful. Don't try to force it.
- Think hard about who is going to read your poem.

WORDS, WORDS, WORDS

For this kind of poem, the lists are made up by 'word association'. That's where one of you says a word and the next person has to say the first word which comes into his or her head.

1. Work in groups of three with two players and one referee. Swap roles as each round finishes.

2. The two players face each other. The referee gives a starting word and players take it in turn to say a single word which must, in some way, be connected with the word before. The round finishes when one player can't offer a word or gives a word which is completely unconnected with the word which went before. The referee's decision on this is final! The referee also acts as secretary, jotting down all the words which are said.

3. After several rounds, your group will have a number of different lists. You can each develop these into list poems in all sorts of ways.
   For example, you might choose to tell a simple story. You can probably guess what the starting word was for the poem by James Pocknell.

Words
Frown
Push
Shove
Aggression
Chants
Slap
Punch
Kick
Cut
Blood
Teacher
Run

James Pocknell

You can also add description to the poem, to make your story more interesting.

Green bush
Leafy tree
Play a game
Eyes closed
Counting slow
1 – 2 – 3
Then faster
7 – 8 – 9
Coming!
Ready or not!
Green Bush
Leafy tree
Found you
You're IT!

Sarah Shore

If the starting word is a colour, your list poems may be more descriptive.

An elephant
A high-rise flat
A road
A wintry sky
My school uniform
A dull day
All these are grey

Jenny Naylor

Red
A sunset
Fresh tulips
A blushing cheek
A velvet rose
A big balloon
A bloody battle

Alison Lee

Another way to develop these list poems is to add words once your line-order has been settled. Add one word to the second line, two to the third and so on. This makes you think hard, and produces a poem with an interesting shape.

Home!
Get changed
Put books away
Run to the park
Meet Jamie, Alice, Andrew, Sam
All clatter up the slide
Sit at the top, very still.

Judith Marchant

Meet a Poet

Edwin Morgan is a well-known poet who enjoys using lists in his poems. Reading how he writes list poems will help you to write your own.

There have always been lists in poetry, as far back as you like to go. It may seem strange that something as formal as a list should be found in a poem. After all, aren't poems supposed to be free, unexpected and unplanned? Aren't they supposed to come from inspiration? I think the answer is yes and no! When I write, there is an element of inspiration, with ideas, images and words flying into my head. I often don't know exactly where they came from, except that they seem right. But I find some poems can also be helped along by giving them a good clear shape or structure that readers can see and enjoy.

One of my poems which uses a list is *The Computer's First Christmas Card*. This was written in 1963 when computers were still quite new. People were experimenting with them to see what they could do. Could they produce poems, stories or music? This poem is my way of commenting on all these activities. It was not written with the help of a computer, and so it is only an imaginary computer poem.

As you can see at once from the way the poem is printed on the page, it is meant to look very rigid and mechanical, as if it had come from a machine. All the lines have the same number of letters, and each line has the same structure.

The idea in the poem is that the computer has been asked to come up with the message for a Christmas card. It goes through its memory bank, and prints out words which all have something to do with the Christmas season of goodwill: people going to parties and enjoying themselves, eating a lot of jelly under the holly and becoming very merry and jolly. At the end, you can see how the pattern of the lines breaks down as the poor computer, doing its best, switches off not with the message MERRY CHRISTMAS which it should have found, but with MERRY CHRYSANTHEMUM. The fact that the computer nearly gets it right but not quite, is meant to show that computer poetry still has some way to go!

The Computer's First Christmas Card
jollymerry
hollyberry
jollyberry
merryholly
happyjolly
jollyjelly
jellybelly
bellymerry
hollyheppy
jollyMolly
marryJerry
merryHarry
hoppyBarry
heppyJarry
boppyheppy
berryjorry
jorryjolly
moppyjelly
Mollymerry
Jerryjolly
bellyboppy
jorryhoppy
hollymoppy
Barrymerry
Jarryhappy
happyboppy
boppyjolly
jollymerry
merrymerry
merrymerry
merryChris
ammerryasa
Chrismerry
asMERRYCHR
YSANTHEMUM

LIST POEMS

My list poem *Off Course*, written in 1966, is one of a group of what I call spacepoems, all of them connected with the exploration of space by the Russians and Americans. I followed this with great interest right from the first sputnik in 1957, and on through the first dog in space, the first man in space, the moon landings, the rocket disasters. When I was at school I loved reading the science fiction magazines of the time, like *Amazing Stories* and *Astounding Stories*. When actual space voyages began to take place, in the 1960s and 1970s, I found I wanted to bring something of all that into my poetry.

With *Off Course*, I wanted to write about a space disaster. But the poem is not about any one actual disaster. It was just the idea of a moon rocket going off course, out of control, and blowing up, with the loss of the people on board, that I wanted to write about. I didn't want to describe the flight in connected detail, like a story. Instead I wanted to have a list of separate images, each one saying something about the expedition: the 'golden flood' of sunlight; the 'smuggled mouth-organ' (this did happen on one of the American flights, and of course any extra weight, even a small weight, could be dangerous); the 'space walk' as members of the crew leave the capsule; the 'lifeline continents' which can still be seen down below.

Then in the second section of the poem (where the seven last lines start further in to show that some change has taken place), I scramble the images to give the idea of something chaotic: the rocket breaking up, the contents and the crew being shattered and cast out into space. At the end all you have is the 'cabin debris' and the 'orbit mouth-organ'.

I think a list of separate images like this can sometimes be a very good way of writing a poem. It is like a series of camera shots, as in a film. You cut from one shot to another. You build up a good picture in the viewer's or reader's mind, without needing to connect the images by saying 'He did this' or 'They remembered that'. You could try this out for yourselves on different subjects.

So – over to you now. Happy listing!

Off Course

the golden flood   the weightless seat
the cabin song   the pitch black
the growing beard   the floating crumb
the shining rendezvous   the orbit wisecrack
the hot spacesuit   the smuggled mouth-organ
the imaginary somersault   the visionary sunrise
the turning continents   the space debris
the golden lifeline   the space walk
the crawling deltas   the camera moon
the pitch velvet   the rough sleep
the crackling headphone   the space silence
the turning earth   the lifeline continents
the cabin sunrise   the hot flood
the shining spacesuit   the growing moon

    the crackling somersault   the smuggled orbit
    the rough moon   the visionary rendezvous
    the weightless headphone   the cabin debris
    the floating lifeline   the pitch sleep
    the crawling camera   the turning silence
    the space crumb   the crackling beard
    the orbit mouth-organ   the floating song

Before you move on to write more list poems of your own, read a list poem called *The Electric Household* written by a poet called Wes Magee. As you can see, he has used word association to write this poem.

Look at how Wes Magee uses rhymes in his poem to keep the rhythm of the poem going. Notice how he orders his electrical goods in unexpected ways. The poem ends with a *pun*. An 'ohm' is an electrical term. He uses it instead of the word 'home' which sounds almost identical and which you would expect to read there. It makes the ending of the poem rather surprising and, perhaps, a little sad.

The Electric Household

cooker blanket
toothbrush fire
iron lightbulb
tv dryer
fridge radio
robot drill
toaster speaker
kettle grill
slicer grinder
meters fan
slide projector
deep fry pan
vacuum cleaner
fuses shocks
freezer shaver
junction box
water heater
time switch lamps
knife recorder
cables amps
door chimes organ
infra red
guitar video
sunlamp bed
heated rollers
current watts
train adaptor
bulkhead spots
synthesizer
night light glow
calculator
stereo
cultivator
metronome
volts hair crimper
ohm sweet ohm

THINGS, THINGS, THINGS

To build this sort of poem, you need to think of lots of different ideas, all suggested by a simple starting point. Here are some possible starting points.

- — Things to do on a wet day in the holidays
- — Things I'm always losing
- — Things I'll never part with
- — Things to say to get out of trouble
- — Things to do when you can't get to sleep
- — Things in my house that nobody notices

Think hard about what to include. For example, the 'things I'm always losing', might not be just exercise books or dinner money. They could also be your temper, time and your childhood.

There are some examples of this type of poem on this page. You should be able to guess what the starting points were.

Count the patterns on the wallpaper
Throw my toys at the ceiling
Go under the bed covers and back up to the top
Bury myself under my pillow
Bang on my ladder
Play with my clock
Read under the covers with my torch
Listen to the television downstairs
The noises of cars
Angie's barks
Stare at the ceiling
Think of school
Say my tables
Throw all my covers off

Judith Wright

It's Saturday
I'm feeling ill
No school today
I'm sleeping still.

I'm just coming
A minute more
Was that someone
At the door?

It's too early
I'm fast asleep
What's for breakfast?
Won't it keep?

Rebecca Sims

I wonder if anyone notices
The mud that's on the floor
The dog hairs on the carpet
And the scratches on the door.

Does anyone ever notice
The chipped surfaces on plates
The rusty dented cake tins
And the dusty iron weights?

Mary Deliyannis

Ask Chris, he never does anything.
I did them yesterday.
I promised Susan I would call for her.
I've got to do my homework.
Was that someone at the door?
Ask Dave, he won't mind.
But Mum, I've got to get changed!
The dog needs a walk.
I must clean the bird-cage out.
I've got a headache.
I feel sick.
My English teacher said I should read my library book.

Vicky Tunstall

Another way to write this sort of list poem, is to use the idea of *where things come from* as your starting point. How about these starting points?

— Where the dark comes from

— Where silence comes from

— Where softness comes from

— Where cold comes from

— Where fear comes from

— Where dryness comes from

— Where a particular colour comes from

— Where loneliness comes from

Be exciting and original with these ideas as well. 'Where cold comes from' could be the fridge, ice and snow, but it could also be an apple's flesh, a teacher's stare, granny's hands, and so on.

QUIET

The classroom
When nobody's there
The house at night
When everyone's asleep
In space by yourself
Underneath the ground
The graveyard at midnight
The early morning sun.

Colette Smith

DARKNESS

A locked cupboard
A turned-out light
Night.

Michael Cheetham

SILENCE

An exam room
On a Monday morning.
A barred window
In a dark prison cell.
Living alone
In a high-rise flat.
An empty box
Telling no story.
Underwater
Below the world.
An ended life
Forever silent.

Penny Clapp

DARK

Dark is silence
Dark is cold
Dark is emptiness
Dark is old

Dark is blindness
Dark is war
Dark is quietness
Dark is poor

Dark is cruelty
Dark is sad
Dark is children
Dark is bad.

Nicola Wheeler

DRYNESS

As dry as the white on a snooker cue,
Sometimes white and sometimes blue;
As dry as the dust on an antique chair,
It's been so long since someone sat there.
As dry as some books dug out from the loft,
With all the pages going soft.
As dry as the fur on a white, purring cat,
You can feel the dryness as you reach down to pat.
As dry as the tongue on a marathon runner,
Finishing the course in the middle of Summer.
As dry as a windmill filled full of corn,
With sails that were turning before you were born.
As dry as the bones in an ancient old tomb,
Completely alone in an eternal room.

Alice Thornton

MAGIC SPELLS

This time you are going to make lists which build up into spells. One of the most famous spells comes from the play *Macbeth* by William Shakespeare. It is spoken by three witches. Here, on the right, is one of the verses.

Now, see how powerful a spell you can write.

1 Working in pairs, decide on the spell you want to cast. Here are some examples to start you thinking:

— A spell to make it rain or stop raining
— A spell to make you grow rich
— A spell to make you better at something
— A spell to make the holiday last longer
— A spell to make your bedroom tidy

2 Once you've decided on the spell, each think of some 'ingredients' and write them down. Use one line for each ingredient and try to make them match the spell you are casting. For example, if you're writing a spell to make it stop raining, then some of the ingredients might be a fluffy cloud, a rainbow's arch or a warm breeze.

3 Now use a pair of scissors to cut the lines into separate strips. Rearrange them into the order that you and your partner agree is best. Read the various possibilities out loud and try them on other pairs before deciding on your final poem.

Fillet of a fenny snake,
In the cauldron boil and bake;
Eye of newt, and toe of frog,
Wool of bat, and tongue of dog,
Adder's fork and blind-worm's sting,
Lizard's leg, and howlet's wing,
For a charm of powerful trouble,
Like a hell broth boil and bubble.

A Spell to Make You Rich

Stir into a magic pot,
O'er a fire – very hot,
Then you'll have a potion which
When drunk, will make you very rich.

The silver moon's midnight ray,
Caught on the finest night in May.
A golden eagle's every toe,
Next into the bowl must go,
Add an empty, pauper's purse –
A worm, to make the taste much worse,
Then a toad's jewelled eye
In the cauldron quickly fry.

A ring snatched from 'twixt bride and groom,
A chip of stone from Midas' tomb,
A sapphire coloured speedwell blue,
Two blades of emerald grass which grew,
'Neath a ruby rose and near
Diamonds of a baby's tear.
Mix in all and last to suit
Your favourite flavoured opal fruit!

Nicola Scott

A spell to Recapture a Perfect Moment

A child's tear,
Wrapped in spider's silvery net.
A velvet blossom,
Plucked cruelly from the tree.
An arrow, fashioned out of gold,
An oyster's cherished pearl,
Long polished by the sea.

A single crystal drop of morning dew,
A violet's humble scent,
Half-captured in a dream.
A heartbeat, hunted by its joy,
A snail's forgotten caravan,
Washed in a meadow stream.

Rebecca Sims

A Spell to put on your Brother

Mud
From the depths of the soccer pitch,
Mould
From the crust of old bread,
Orange juice
From the back of the cupboard,
Engine oil
Fresh off the garage floor.
Mix them together nice and quick, then
Down his back
All gungy and thick.

Gary Moment

A Shrinking Spell

A little tin,
A tiny pin,
A strike of a match,
A tint of gold,
Half of a ring,
A robin's wing.

Kathryn Gallimore

Collect and keep your poems

Collect all your poems together into one anthology (the name for a collection of poems). You could use this for a class display or you could keep it, adding other poems as you try other activities later in this book.

Tips for Success

- Use lots of original ideas.
- Edit them carefully into the best order.
- Add descriptive words whenever you can.
- Use a mixture of line lengths and arrange your words to give your poem a good rhythm.
- Use unusual rhymes or repeated phrases.
- Read your poem out loud to check the rhyme and rhythm.

Reading Aloud

Sometimes you may want to read a magazine or a book quietly to yourself. Sometimes reading a poem or a story out loud, with other people, can help you understand it better and enjoy it more. In this unit you will have the chance to practise reading a poem and a story aloud.

you will be....

- Solving problems
- Reading aloud

Now read on...

The passage on the opposite page will make you think hard about your reading.

FIRST

Read the passage to yourself several times and try to work out what words should go in each of the gaps. Looking forward and backwards in the passage will help you do this. If you are not sure of a particular word, go on and then come back to it. This is exactly what you would have to do if you were reading a very difficult book or some hard-to-follow instructions.

THEN

In groups of three or four, compare the words you have thought of. Many will be obvious but some you will have to discuss among yourselves. Between you, try to choose the *best* answer – the word which most of you think fits best.

FINALLY

Present your list to the class and compare it with those that other groups have come up with. You'll be quite surprised at some of the differences!

Why read aloud?

EVERYONE needs to learn to read –1– as well as they can. We obtain much of the –2– we need by reading: reading newspapers, advertisements, or instructions. We can also get a lot of –3– from reading good stories or interesting articles. Reading is one of the most –4– –5– you can learn. Schools can help everyone –6– their reading. Just as you learn to ride a bike by riding, wobbling along until you no longer –7– off, so you improve your reading by –8–. Practice, practice, and more –9– makes perfect.

YOU may sometimes be asked to read –10– in class. This can be good fun if you are reading something you like, but some people find it –11–. It is important that the –12– class helps those who find it difficult. Everyone can then become more confident. How can you help? By –13– calling out as soon as the reader –14–. Very often the reader can work out the word if you give her time. If you interrupt immediately you make her think she cannot do it by herself. You take away her –15–. If you are –16– for a moment, and she manages to read it, you will have helped her become a tiny bit more confident. Let the –17– decide when help is needed. Then the next time she is –18– to read aloud, it will be –19– for her.

WHEN you read aloud, you should do more than just –20– the words. You must try to make the passage come alive for your listener. The flat –21– on the page have to turn into a living and interesting story. You can do this by –22– your voice. You can make it go up and down, faster and –23–, louder and softer. If you put life into your voice in this way, you can make the exciting bits more exciting, the funny bits –24–, and the whole thing becomes more entertaining for your listeners.

EVEN a –25– reader, may find some reading material –26– at some point in his –27–. But the great thing about learning to read –28– is that it is a skill you never lose once you have –29– it. In a few years time, you will be reading stories aloud to your children and they may then –30– even better readers than you!

The power of the spoken word

You are now going to read the story below out loud and you'll start to see the power of the spoken word. There won't be a dry eye in the classroom!

The story is called *Lasca* and it is told by a cowboy. He tells of a time when he tried to rescue a Mexican woman called Lasca from a cattle stampede. The Texas 'Norther' which he mentions is a wind which upsets cattle. 'Steed' and 'Mustang' are both names for a horse. 'Coyote' (a desert wolf) is pronounced 'coyottee'.

On your own
Read the story through quietly on your own so that you get a general idea of what it is about.

In pairs
Join together with a partner and practise reading the story out loud. Decide how you want to share the reading. When will you change reader?

You will need to practise reading the story several times. The punctuation marks will help tell you when to pause and take a

LASCA

BY F. DESPREZ

One night when the air was hot, I sat by her side and forgot – forgot! Forgot the herd that were taking their rest. Forgot that the air was close opprest. Forgot that the Texas 'Norther' comes sudden and soon, in the dead of night or the blaze of noon. Once let the herd at its breath take flight, nothing on earth can stop their flight. Then woe to the rider, and woe to the steed, who falls in front of their mad stampede!

Was that thunder? I grasped the cord of my swift mustang without a word. I sprang to the saddle – and she clung behind. Away on a hot chase down the wind! Never was fox hunt half so hard, and never was steed so little spared. We rode for our lives. You shall hear how we fared – in Texas, down by the Rio Grande.

The mustang flew and we urged him on. There was one chance left – and you have but one. Halt, jump to the ground and shoot your horse. Crouch under his carcass and take your chance. And if the steers in their frantic course, don't batter you both to pieces at once, you may thank your stars. If not, goodbye to the quickening kiss, the long drawn sigh, the open air, and the open sky – in Texas, down by the Rio Grande.

The cattle gained on us. Just as I felt for my old six shooter behind in my belt, down came the mustang, and down came we, clinging together. What was the rest? A body that spread itself on my breast. Two arms that shielded my dizzy head, two lips that hard on my lips were prest. Then came thunder in my ears, as over us surged the sea of steers. Blows beat blood into my eyes and when I could rise – Lasca was dead!

I gouged out a grave a few feet deep, and there in the earth's arms I laid her to sleep. And there she is lying and no one knows. The summer shines and the winter snows. The little grey hawk hangs aloft in the air. The sly coyote trots here and there. The black snake glides and glitters and slides into a hole in a cottonwood tree. The buzzard sails on and comes and is gone, stately and still like a ship at sea. And I wonder why I do not care for the things that are, like the things that were. Does half my heart lie buried there – in Texas, down by the Rio Grande?

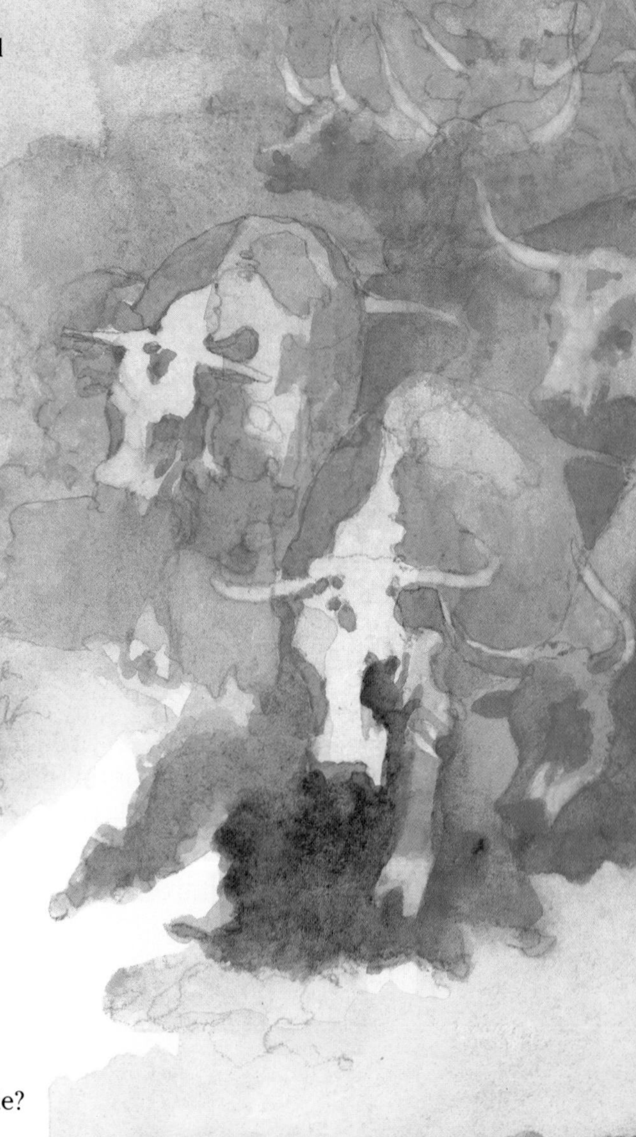

breath. Some parts of the story may need to be faster and louder than others. In some parts you need to be able to get across the rhythm of hoofbeats in the words.

In groups
When you are happy with the way you are reading the story, join together with another pair. Read the story aloud to each other. Discuss what the differences in the readings were. Whose reading was most enjoyable? Perhaps they were equally good, but in different ways.

Tips for Success

- Read the whole passage through carefully before you start.
- Decide when to change reader.
- Decide where to vary the speed.

Reading poems aloud

Reading a poem aloud is very similar to reading a story. Again, the important thing is to make the poem come to life for your listener. Again, you need to read with as much expression as possible.

This time, get into small groups and practise reading the poem on this page together. Think about these questions:

- Does reading the poem aloud, make it more interesting than reading it silently to yourself? Why do you think this is?
- Does it help having different readers? When is it best to change reader?

The Inchcape Rock

No stir in the air, no stir in the sea;
The ship was still as she could be;
Her sails from heaven received no motion;
Her keel was steady in the ocean.

Without either sign or sound of their shock,
The waves flowed over the Inchcape Rock;
So little they rose, so little they fell,
They did not move the Inchcape Bell.

The worthy Abbot of Aberbrothok
Had placed that bell on the Inchcape Rock;
On a buoy in the storm it floated and swung,
And over the waves its warning rung.

When the rock was hid by the surge's swell,
The mariners heard the warning bell;
And then they knew the perilous rock,
And blest the Abbot of Aberbrothok.

The sun in heaven was shining gay,
All things were joyful on that day;
The sea birds screamed as they wheeled around,
And there was joyance in their sound.

The buoy of the Inchcape Bell was seen,
A darker speck on the ocean green.
Sir Ralph the Rover walked his deck,
And he fixed his eye on the darker speck.

He felt the cheering power of Spring;
It made him whistle; it made him sing;
His heart was mirthful to excess;
But the Rover's mirth was wickedness.

His eye was on the Inchcape float;
Quoth he, 'My men, put out the boat,
And row me to the Inchcape Rock,
And I'll plague the Abbot of Aberbrothok.'

The boat is lowered; the boatmen row,
And to the Inchcape Rock they go.
Sir Ralph bent over from the boat,
And he cut the bell from the Inchcape float.

Down sank the bell with a gurgling sound;
The bubbles rose and burst around.
Quoth Sir Ralph, 'The next who comes to the Rock
Won't bless the Abbot of Aberbrothok.'

Sir Ralph the Rover sailed away;
He scoured the seas for many a day;
And now, grown rich with plundered store,
He steers his course for Scotland's shore.

So thick a haze o'erspreads the sky
They cannot see the sun on high;
The wind hath blown a gale all day;
At evening it hath died away.

On deck the Rover takes his stand;
So dark it is they see no land.
Quoth Sir Ralph, 'It will be lighter soon;
For there is the dawn of the rising moon.'

'Canst hear,' said one, 'the breaker's roar?
For methinks we should be near the shore.'
'Now where we are I cannot tell;
But I wish I could hear the Inchcape Bell!'

They hear no sound; the swell is strong;
Though the wind hath fallen they drift along,
Till the vessel strikes with a shivering shock, –
'Oh heavens! It is the Inchcape Rock!'

Sir Ralph the Rover tore his hair;
He cursed himself in his despair.
The waves rush in on every side;
The ship is sinking beneath the tide.

But even now, in his dying fear
One dreadful sound could the Rover hear –
A sound as if, with the Inchcape Bell,
The fiends in triumph were ringing his knell.

Robert Southey

- Do you need to vary the speed of the reading? Where? Why?
- Are there verses which need to be read more loudly/more softly than the others? Which?

You might like to try reading the poem aloud at home to a younger sister or brother. They are your audience. You want them to enjoy the poem and be gripped by it, right to the end. Can you do this?

HEADLINE NEWS!

Every day, in any newspaper, there are probably fifty or sixty different headlines. This unit looks at how headlines are used to give readers information and to encourage them to read the story underneath.

The headlines and stories on these pages are from a selection of newspapers published on the day after the birth of a baby girl to the Duchess of York.

you will be....

- **Giving an opinion**
- **Reporting on discussion**

Looking at headlines

Working in pairs, look at the headlines on these pages and decide:

- Which headline gives the most information.
- Which headline you think is the most striking. Why?
- Which headline you like best. Why?
- Which of the sub-headings is most informative. Which one catches your attention best.

Reading the stories

The beginnings of all the news stories on the royal birth contain very similar information because the newspapers were all given the same press statement. Read them carefully and then, in pairs, choose *two* of the stories to compare. Each choose one of these and look more closely at it.

1. Look at the facts. What does the newspaper tell you, the reader, about the birth? Make a list of the information which is given in the story *in the order in which it is given*.
2. Compare your story with your partner's. Which account gives more information? How similar is the information in the two stories? Is there information in one story which is not given in the other?
3. 'Skim' read the other stories for information which only they contain. Which papers 'seem' to know more about the birth?
4. Report back to the class, or another pair, on what you have found out.

IT'S a girl! Fergie ended the waiting game of the year when she finally gave birth to a daughter last night.

And proud Prince Andrew was at her side to share the magic moment.

The message the world had waited to hear was finally posted on the gates of Buckingham Palace.

Crowds outside the Palace and London's luxury Portland Hospital greeted the news with a roar of delight.

The baby is hotly tipped to be given the name Annabel.

The Princess of York was born at 8.18 p.m. (on the 8th of the 8th '88) and weighed 6lb 12oz.

It was a magical, mystical date celebrated by loving couples all over the world who chose it as their wedding day.

Star

FERGIE gave birth to a bouncing baby girl last night.

Overjoyed Prince Andrew was at his wife's side for the arrival of their 6lb 12oz daughter.

The baby's arrival at 8.18pm on the eighth day of the eighth month of 1988 delighted millions of excited royal fans.

Cheers

News of the arrival drew a huge cheer from crowds packing the pavements around London's Portland Hospital.

Many had stood there in sweltering temperatures since early morning when Andrew drove his wife to her £350-a-day maternity suite.

Buckingham Palace said everything had gone well but a spokesman would not reveal whether the birth had been induced.

Daily Mirror

The Duchess of York last night gave birth safely to a baby daughter, who immediately becomes fifth in line to the throne.

The baby will be known as Princess (Name) of York.

With her husband the Duke of York at her side, the Duchess gave birth to a girl weighing 6lb 12oz at 8.18 pm last night in the Portland private hospital in London, a little more than five hours after she went into labour. The news was announced to the Press Association, and in traditional fashion by the posting of a notice on the railings of Buckingham Palace.

A Palace spokesman also made the announcement to a throng of several hundred newsmen and curious tourists waiting outside the hospital. The crowd immediately raised three cheers.

The Times

LUC
FOR

Tyre
anxiou
Fergie

At 8.18 on 8.8.88 – a safe and lucky Royal birth

The Times

IT'S A GIRL!

Beaming . . proud father Prince Andrew leaves Portland Hospital after a great night Picture: ARTHUR EDWARDS

ROYAL BABY Sun

Sun

Sun

Y GIRL -ERGIE

Today

HIP, hip, hooray! The Duchess of York gave birth to a baby girl last night.

Amazingly, the little lass arrived at **8.18pm** on the **EIGHTH** day of the **EIGHTH** month of **1988**. She weighed 6lb 12oz.

Husband Prince Andrew was there to see his daughter arrive after Fergie went into labour in the early evening.

And vast crowds waiting outside London's Portland Hospital and Buckingham Palace greeted the news with a chorus of cheers.

A Palace bulletin said: "Her Royal Highness and her child are both well."

The baby girl is the delighted royal couple's first child and becomes fifth in line to the throne.

Fergie's gynaecologist, Mr Anthony Kenney, induced the birth shortly after the Duchess was admitted to London's Portland Hospital at 10am.

Sun

●Born: 8.18 on 8/8/88
●Baby weighs 6lb 12oz
●Andrew sees the birth

Sun

A daughter for the Duke and Duchess of York

The Times

creech as uke drives to hospital

Daily Mail

SPEED DELIVERY!

Daily Mail

Now Meet a Headline Writer

When you read a headline, think about the planning and thought that went into it. George Lynn works for the *Sun* newspaper. On the right is his account of how the headline on the previous page was written.

1 Read the two stories from the *Daily Mail*. Use what you have learned to make up your own headlines for each story.

2 In groups, compare your headlines.
— Are they the same? What are the main differences?
— Which do you think is most likely to capture a reader's attention? Why?
— Are your headlines closely linked to the information contained in the report itself? Does it matter, as long as the headline catches the eye?

Remember

- Headlines don't have to be written in sentences. They often leave out words to make them shorter and snappier.
- Headlines are often jokes or puns which can be understood in two ways.
- Headlines don't always refer to the main point of the story. They will often focus on the most eye-catching fact, rather than the most important information.

The reason the headline was chosen was that it answers the first question everyone asks when a baby is born: Is it a boy or girl? It was also the easiest headline to prepare in advance.

We could not know when the baby would be born and this could have occurred close to the time when The Sun goes to press when page changes have to be made rapidly.

We therefore prepared the entire front page announcing the Royal birth well before the event. An identical one was also prepared in case the baby had been a boy. The headline would then have been 'It's a boy!'.

The bulk of the news story was also prepared in advance, leaving space for details such as the baby's weight which would be known only after the birth.

George Lynn
Editorial Executive

By JOHN HAMSHIRE

WELL, their orders were clear enough. 'Pitch a tent in the most unusual or challenging location you can think of and stay there for 21 hours.'

That is why these Venture Scouts set up camp (pictured below) at the top of Britain's second tallest chimney — the 244 metres high power station stack on the Isle of Grain in Kent.

The idea was part of the Venture Scout movement's 21st birthday celebrations this year.

The first problem was actually getting there — up 1,066 leg-wearying steps. That alone took the eight boys and three girls from Edenbridge, Kent, more than half an hour.

But once up, said 16-year-old Nick Martin, 'the weather was perfect, not at all cold and no wind. We had tremendous visibility and could see London 20 miles away'.

The chimney is only 15 metres shorter than Britain's tallest chimney at Drax power station in Yorkshire.

Daily Mail

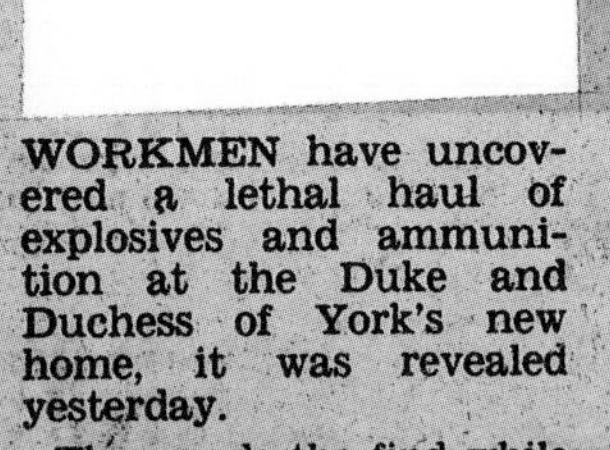

WORKMEN have uncovered a lethal haul of explosives and ammunition at the Duke and Duchess of York's new home, it was revealed yesterday.

They made the find while draining a lake during renovation in the five-acre grounds of the planned £5million mansion near Windsor Castle.

The haul amounts to at least 100 shells and live ammunition — and a rusting armoured jeep — thought to have been left behind by American servicemen who used Sunninghill Park as a training base during World War II.

Daily Mail

Getting around

In this unit you are asked to give, and listen to, instructions and directions. These are important skills which you can easily improve with practice.

you will be . . . .

- Giving directions
- Following instructions
- Giving directions

Getting started

1 Work in pairs. Think of somewhere in the school you would like another pair to travel to, starting from the room you are in.

2 Work out directions which will help the other pair to arrive at that destination. (You must assume that they have no knowledge of the school whatsoever. They do not know where anything is or what different rooms are called.)

3 Join with another pair. Give them your directions. Allow yourselves only one minute. If your directions are clear, they should quickly be able to discover the place where you want them to go. They can then give you their directions in the same way. You can, of course, ask each other questions during the minute.

Now . . .

4 Discuss as a foursome whose directions were the most helpful. Decide which of these things is *most* important when giving directions. Number them 1–4 in order of importance:

— Giving directions in the right order.

— Giving the person you are talking to a chance to ask you questions.

— Using plenty of description.

— Knowing the area very well yourself.

Mind-walking

Get into small groups. One person in the group gives a series of directions. The rest of the group must shut their eyes and try to visualise in their minds where the 'walker' is going. He or she can ask questions as the mind-walk goes on. For example:

'I am walking out of the school gates, down to the roundabout and turning right. I walk along for about 100 metres. There is a letter box on my immediate left. What is the name of the shop on the other side of the road?'

This is an easy example. With practice you will be able to travel far across town or country!

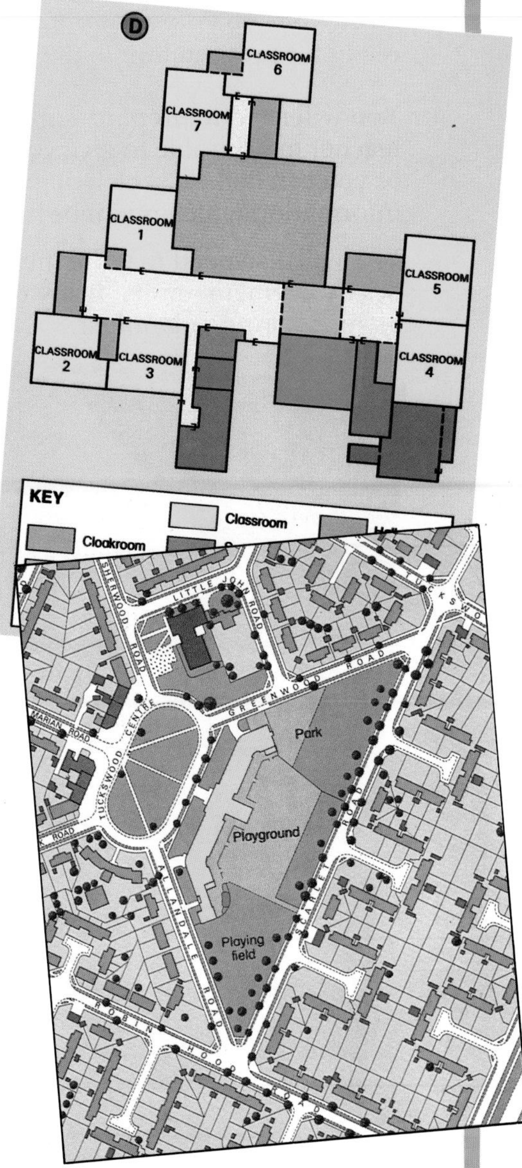

A sponsored Fun Run

Look at the street map opposite. Find Southam High School in square A1. The school wants to organise a sponsored Fun Run and the Deputy Head has asked pupils to help with planning the route.

All runners will be asked to run at least 3 kilometres but no one will be allowed to do more than 24 kilometres. The busy A423 has to be avoided as much as possible.

1. Begin by working on your own. Use the map to plan a possible route.

2. Now join with a partner. Give one another directions which allow both routes to be followed on the map.

3. Decide together on the **best possible** route.

4. Now work up your route and directions into a fully finished form, ready for presentation to the Deputy Head.

- You will need to prepare a map with your route marked on it. Your teacher may be able to give you a photocopy of the map opposite, or you can make a sketch map showing the route and any other information which might be helpful.
- You will also need to write the route directions down clearly and briefly. Remember that if any of the runners get lost, they will blame the route planners!

Tips for Success

Good directions should be:

- clearly expressed in simple language
- detailed enough to avoid confusion
- ordered very carefully
- illustrated where necessary

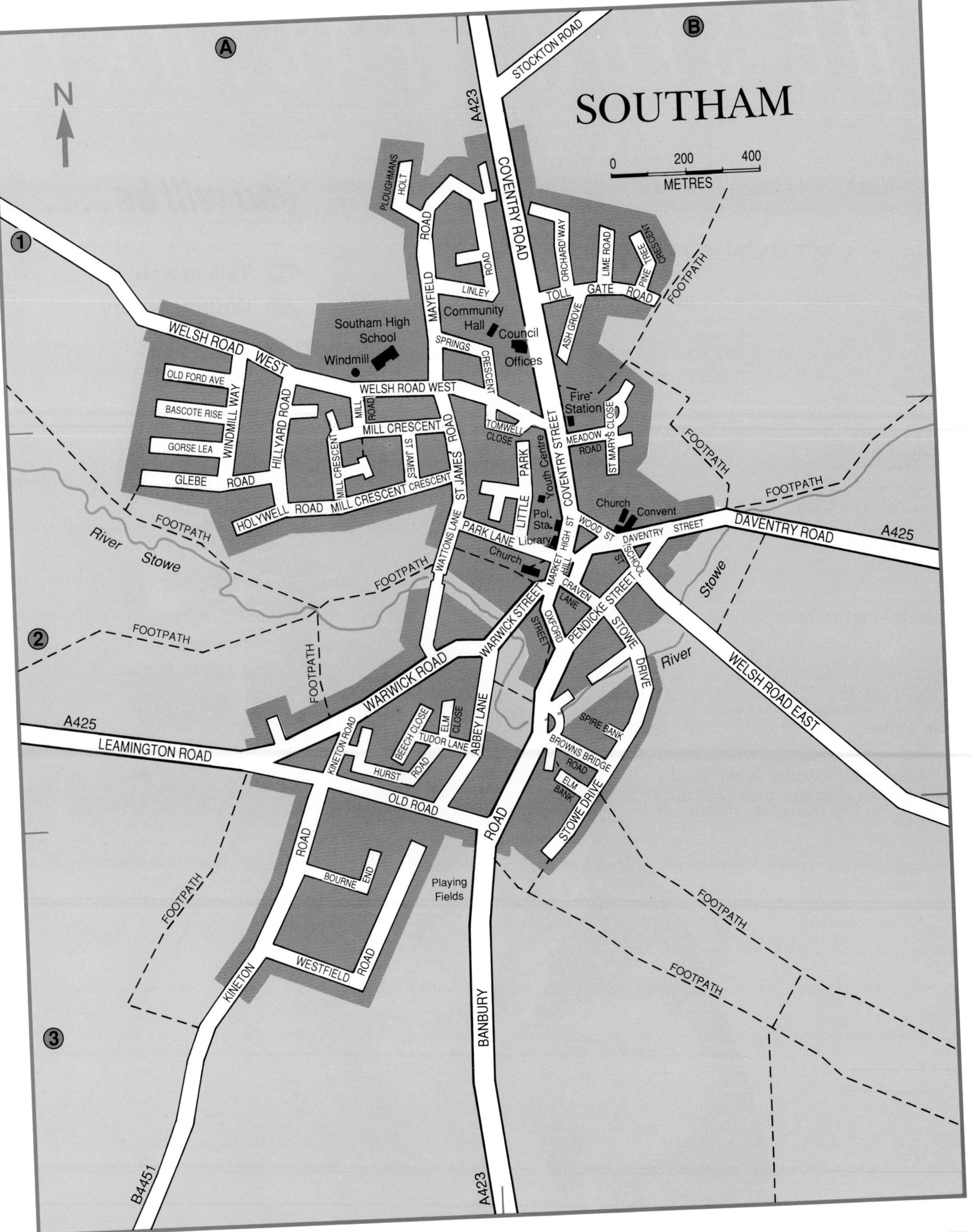
SOUTHAM
N
0
200
400
METRES
A
B
1
2
3
STOCKTON ROAD
A423
COVENTRY ROAD
PLOUGHMANS HOLT
MAYFIELD ROAD
LINLEY ROAD
ORCHARD WAY
LIME ROAD
PINE TREE CRESCENT
TOLL GATE ROAD
ASH GROVE
FOOTPATH
Community Hall
Council Offices
Southam High School
Windmill
WELSH ROAD WEST
SPRINGS CRESCENT
OLD FORD AVE
BASCOTE RISE
GORSE LEA
WINDMILL WAY
HILLYARD ROAD
GLEBE ROAD
MILL ROAD
MILL CRESCENT
ST JAMES CRESCENT
ST JAMES ROAD
TOMWELL CLOSE
Fire Station
MEADOW ROAD
ST MARY'S CLOSE
COVENTRY STREET
Youth Centre
LITTLE PARK
HOLYWELL ROAD
Church
Convent
DAVENTRY ROAD
A425
DAVENTRY STREET
WOOD ST
HIGH ST
Pol. Sta.
Library
PARK LANE
WATTONS LANE
River Stowe
MARKET HILL
SCHOOL ST
CRAVEN LANE
PENDICKE STREET
OXFORD STREET
WARWICK STREET
STOWE DRIVE
WELSH ROAD EAST
WARWICK ROAD
LEAMINGTON ROAD
KINETON ROAD
BEECH CLOSE
ELM CLOSE
TUDOR LANE
ABBEY LANE
HURST ROAD
OLD ROAD
SPIRE BANK
BROWNS BRIDGE ROAD
ELM BANK
BANBURY ROAD
BOURNE END
Playing Fields
WESTFIELD ROAD
KINETON ROAD
B4451

THE STORY FACTORY

This unit looks at some of the ingredients which are used to create stories. It asks you to decide what *you* think makes a good story.

you will be....

- Telling a story
- Writing a story

THE STORYBOARD GAME

- In this activity you start by playing a game and finish by telling a story.
- The purpose of the game is to end up with six elements or ingredients which you will then use to create a story. The six ingredients are:

a character

a setting or location

an object

another character

a chance happening

an ending

- Divide into groups of six, read the rules opposite and play the game.

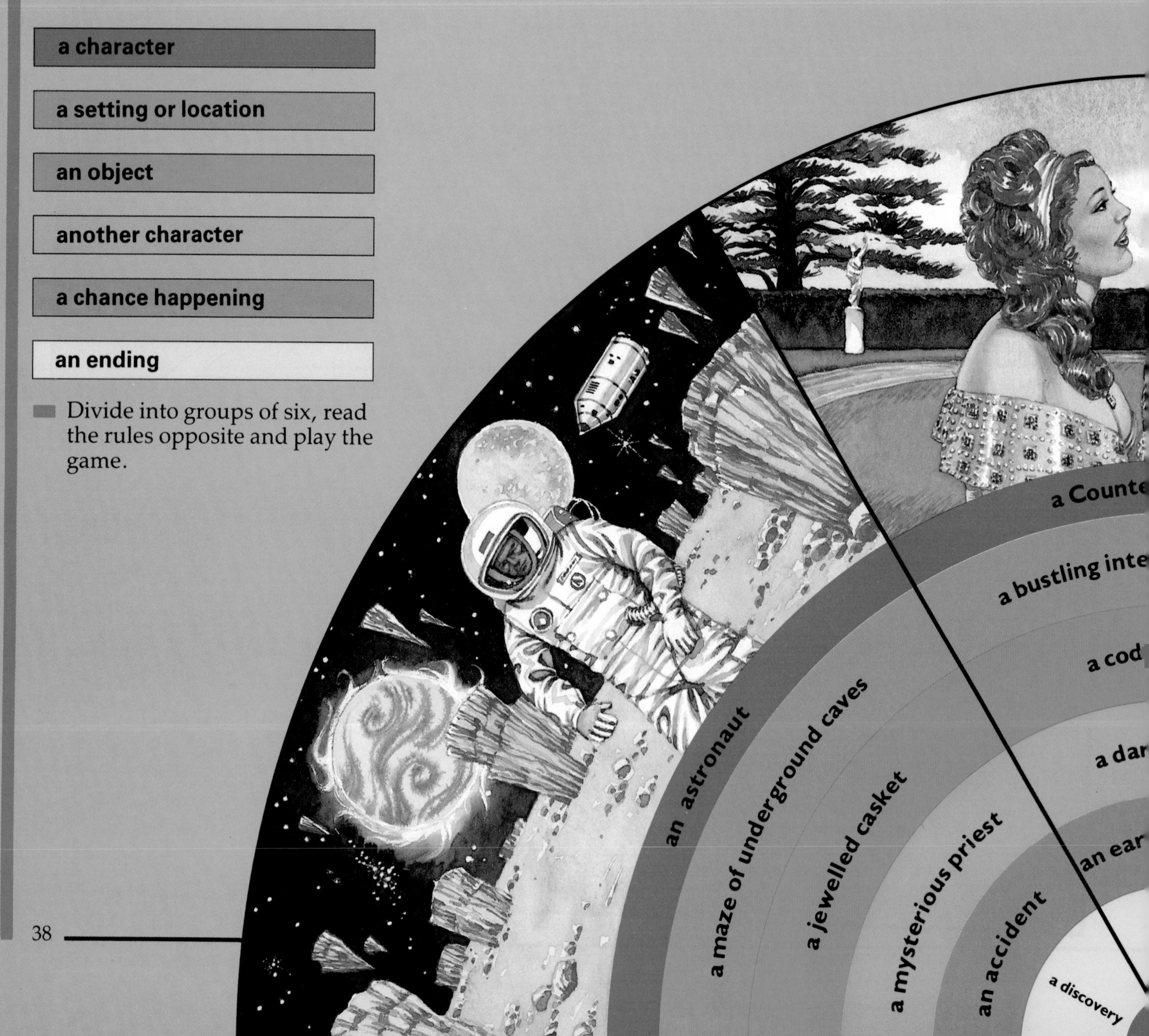

THE RULES

1 Sit around a table with two books arranged to give you the complete board.
2 Throw the dice. The player with the highest score is the Count or Countess. Move the books to face him or her. The other players are the characters nearest to them when the books are moved.
3 Each player throws the dice in turn and counts the number of moves clockwise around the blue circle. The place where he or she lands is the location or setting for the story.
4 Do this four more times, each time moving one band towards the centre of the circle so that you land on an object, another character, a chance happening and an ending. Note down each of the elements as you land on it.
5 The game ends when the last player has collected the five story elements – plus the character they started as.

Note: You can land on the same spot as another player and both use the same element in your story.

NOW CREATE A STORY

- Study the list of ingredients that you've written down. You now have to use your imagination to build them into a short story as cleverly as possible.
- Plan your story. Jot down notes if you want to. The elements can be in any order in your story.
- Arrange your chairs for a group storytelling session. Tell each other, in turn, the stories you've made up.

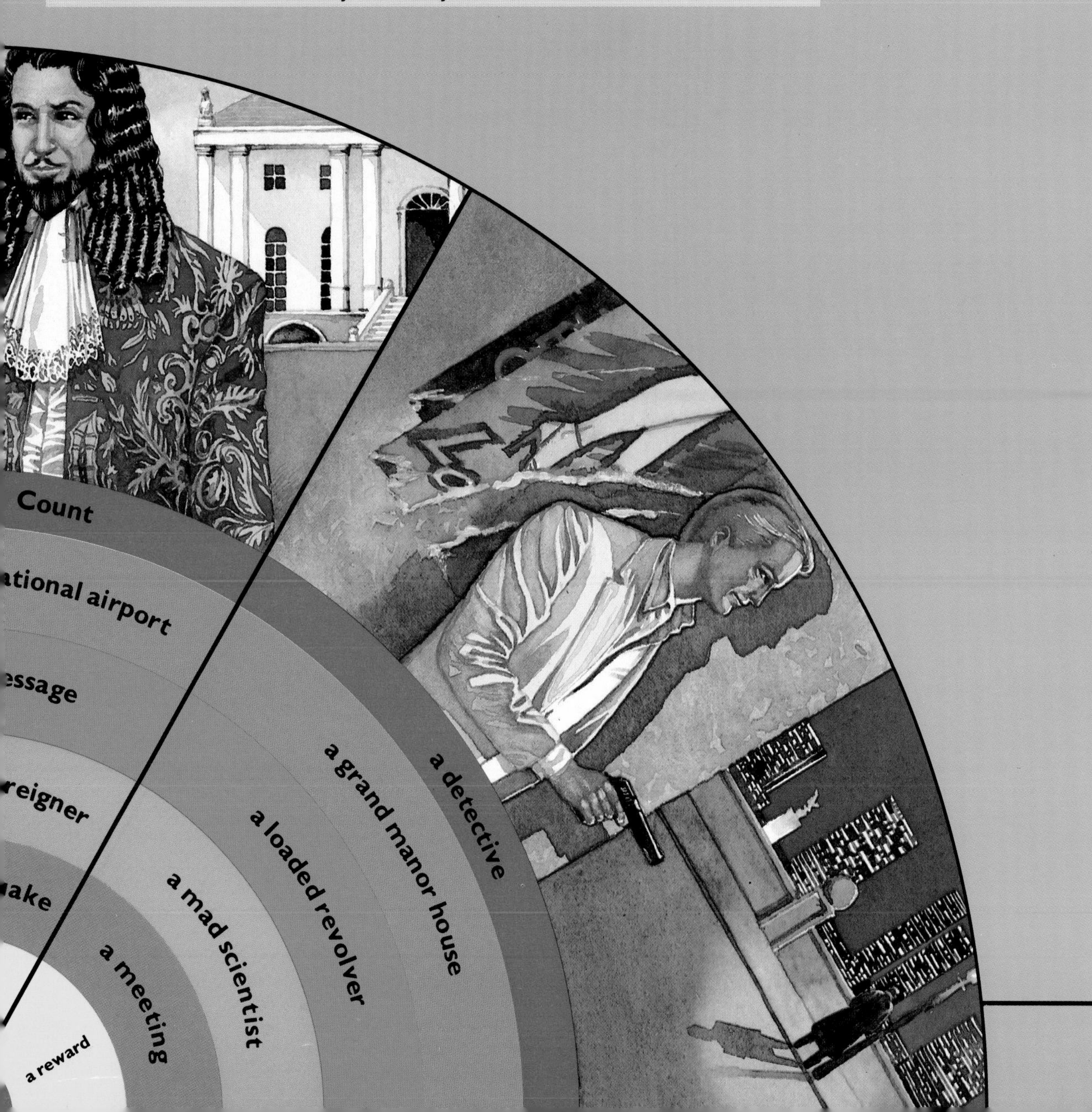

WHAT MAKES A GOOD STORY?

Each group now has to choose just one of the stories for a whole class storytelling session. Before you do this, you'll need to decide what makes a good story. You'll need to think about these questions:

— How easily did the storyteller fit in the six ingredients?

— Did each stage follow on naturally from the one before?

— Did the storyteller hesitate between each stage?

— Was the story long enough?

— Was the ending natural? Surprising? Dull? Obvious?

— Did you enjoy listening to the story or did your attention wander?

Once you have decided which story should be told to the class, the whole group can put forward ideas as to how it can be made even better.

Tips for Success

- Decide what the broad plot of your story is going to be.
- Be imaginative about how you link the elements. Don't make the links too obvious.
- Add as much detail and description as you can.

STORYBOARD PLUS

Once you have told your story, that doesn't have to be the end of it.

- You could write down your story. What changes do you need to make when you write it down? You may have to make clearer what is happening or who is talking.
- Using the elements of the Storyboard Game you could make up one of these different types of stories:

  — a crime thriller
  — an historical romance
  — a science fiction story
  — a spy story
  — a 'Famous Five' type adventure
  — a ghost story

The game deliberately mixes up the ingredients for these different kinds of stories but they are all there on the board.

All you have to do is decide which type or 'genre' of story you want to write. Then pick out from the board the six ingredients which you think fit *best* into this type of story. If you decide on a spy story, for example, you might choose to include:

— a secret agent
— a city centre at night
— a coded message
— a mad scientist
— a murder
— an escape

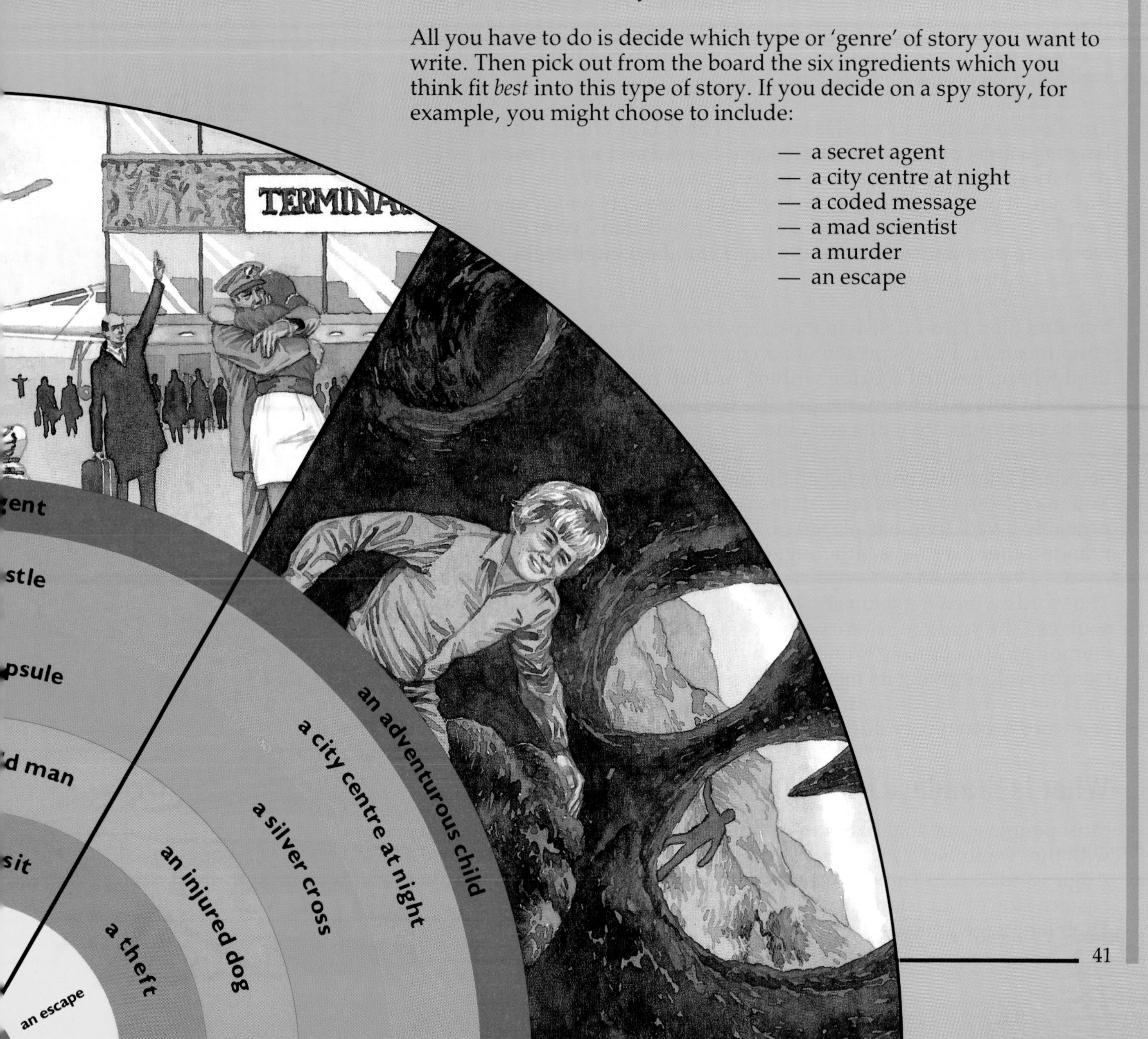

Web of Languages

In this unit you will be finding out where the English language came from. You will also be exploring the many different languages spoken in Britain today.

On your own, in pairs, or as a class read through the information which follows.

you will be....

Locating and selecting information

Presenting information

Many people, many languages

Most people in Britain can talk in more than one language. They may be able to say a few words of French or German remembered from their schooldays. They may go to evening classes to learn Spanish, ready for a holiday. They may be able to speak two languages really well – in which case they are bilingual.

This book is written in what is known as Standard English. It is the language most of you will have learned to read and write first in primary school. It is a different language from, say, Welsh, French or Russian. It is also different from the English dialects which many people speak in the different regions of Great Britain. With dialects, words are pronounced differently from Standard English and some words are also spelt differently.

You find Standard English in most newspapers. It is spoken by announcers and news presenters on national television. It has to be used wherever what is being written, or said, needs to be understood clearly by lots of different people. It is the language we can most easily use to communicate with each other.

Standard English is changing all the time. New words come and go. You may listen to music on a 'stereo cassette recorder' but your mother probably 'jived' to music played on 'a record player'. Your grandmother may have 'jitterbugged' to the 'gramophone'!

The words which make up any language come from all sorts of sources. The study of where words come from is called *etymology*. An etymological dictionary is one which tells you where a word comes from as well as giving its meaning. Languages are constantly changing and borrowing words from one another, so finding the starting point of a word is often very difficult.

What is Standard English?

Most people agree that Standard English, as we know it today, started with the Anglo-Saxon invasions which took place around AD450. The Angles and Saxons came from Northern Europe and settled on the Eastern side of our island, called England (Angle-Land) after them. Their language gradually spread across to the west.

Before the coming of the Anglo-Saxons, the major language spoken was called Celtic. The Celts were the first inhabitants of Britain whose language we know something about. Varieties of the Celtic language are still spoken in outlying and western parts of the British Isles where the Saxons never settled. Welsh is a Celtic language and so is Gaelic which is still spoken by some people in Western Scotland and Ireland. Cornish is another Celtic language.

A surprising number of words we still use today came from Anglo-Saxon, or Old English as it is called. Many place-names are Anglo-Saxon.

ANGLO-SAXON PLACE-NAMES

-ton = village
-stead = large farm
-ham = farm
-ing = followers of
-stock or **-stoke** = cattle farm
-field = farm land surrounded by woods or heath
-ly, or **-ley**, or **-leigh** = clearing among woods or heath

Mucking, therefore, means the place where the followers of Mucca (a Saxon chief) lived.

Ashton means a village by ash trees.

Old English was soon being changed, however, by a new set of words brought from Scandinavia to North-Eastern England by the Vikings. These words were from a separate language called Old Norse and began to come into Old English between AD800 and 900.

William the Conqueror then invaded England from France in 1066 and defeated the English King Harold at the Battle of Hastings. The Normans, as they were known, spoke French of course, and Latin – the language of the Romans who had invaded France before invading England in 55BC.

The Normans had an important influence on the English language for two reasons. First, they settled permanently in England and, secondly, after the Norman invasion, language started to be written down more as well as spoken. For a while, French was the official language used by the ruling Normans, Latin was the language of religion, and Old English was still spoken by the mass of the people. Over the next three hundred years all these joined together into Middle English – a version of Old English but with Norse, French and Latin words added. Although Standard English has changed enormously since then, these languages remain its basic ingredients.

It's important to realise that none of this happened overnight. People didn't wake up one day and talk a different language. In fact, words spread and changed, just as they do today, but over very long periods of time. As English-speaking people travelled, they came across other languages and brought words back into English. There are, for example, many words in English which were originally Dutch because there was a lot of trade with Holland.

Who else has influenced Standard English? The Greeks were conquered by the Romans who spoke Latin. The Latin language adopted some Greek words, so that there are now words of Greek origin in English. England had a colonial empire in Africa and India and many words from languages spoken in these colonies came into Standard English.

Space travel, computing, entertainment and fashion have all produced new words to add to Standard English. The word *video* comes from the Latin 'videre' which means 'to see'. The word *cassette* is from the French for a little box.

Other new words have come from the names of people who invented or discovered them. The Earl of Sandwich liked to cut his bread in half and slip slices of beef inside it. There was also a Mr Hoover, a Duke of Wellington, a Mr Diesel, a Madame Curie, and a Mr Guillotine.

Thinking about what you've read

On your own

The passage you've read contains a lot of information about Standard English. After reading it through once you should 'skim' read it again.

SKIMMING is the name given to a kind of reading which looks quickly through a passage to find out what it is saying *in general*. It misses out the detailed information but tries to get an idea of what the whole thing is about.

Skim read the passage again and say whether the statements on the right are true or false.

- The Greeks once invaded Britain.
- Middle English developed from a mixture of languages including Norse and Latin.
- Gaelic is spoken in isolated parts of Eastern Britain.
- There are some words from the Dutch language in English.
- The Duke of Wellington's family are named after an article of footwear.

SCANNING is a different kind of reading which looks for more *detailed* information. This sort of reading searches for clues which may be just one word long.

Scan the passage to answer the questions below. Finding the underlined words in the passage will help you know where the information you need is:

- What happened in 55BC?
- Where did the Vikings come from?
- What is the Latin word for to see?

Now, look closely at the passage and complete these tasks.

1. On a map of Europe, draw arrows showing which countries brought their words and languages to England – and when. Your teacher will supply you with an outline map.

2. Describe, in five or six sentences, why and how languages change.

Working with a partner

1. Use an etymological dictionary to find out what these things are and where the words for them came from:

   cardigan braille derrick nicotine dolby balaclava hamburger

2. Think of twenty words we use today which your grandparents would not have understood or known when they were your age.

3. Use your dictionary to look up where the words on the right come from. Group them according to the languages they come from. You should find at least five languages.

Alphabet
animal
avalanche
badger
ballet
bungalow
confetti
coracle
cycle
deck
dungarees
exit
fungus
garage
January
knapsack
medium
pyjamas
ragged
skin
stiletto
television
Thursday
ugly
umbrella
volcano
waggon
whisky

Other languages

Apart from Standard English, many other languages are spoken in Britain. Making a language web is one way to find out how many languages you, your relatives and your friends speak.

Making a language web

1 Complete a web like the one shown here. Put your name at the centre and the languages you speak. Then add people you know and their languages. Finally, you can add people they know and the languages that they speak. You'll soon see that just by thinking of your relatives and friends the language web becomes quite varied.

Tips for Success

If you want to understand more about the English Language . . .

- Whenever you look a word up in your dictionary, look at where it comes from.
- Use history textbooks and encyclopedias to find out more about the people who settled in Britain.
- When you study a foreign language, look out for words which are similar to English words.

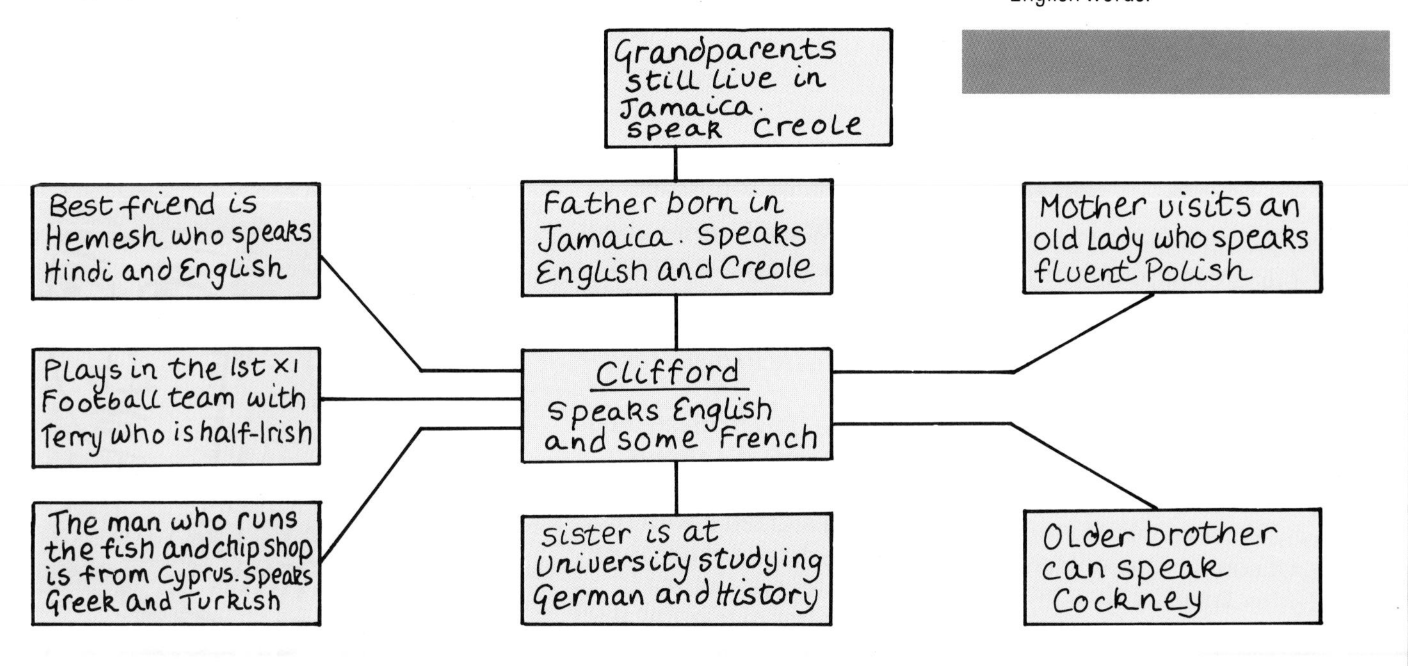

2 You can include dialects and other forms of English such as Australian and American.

Here are some of the languages you are likely to find in your web:

But even these languages have many different forms. Many people from Bengal actually speak a language called Sylheti which is different in a number of ways from Bengali. There are a whole range of Chinese languages including Cantonese and Hokkien. African languages include Ibo, Yoruba and Swahili. Also, as in Britain, different regions have different dialects and accents. A French Canadian speaker sounds quite different from a Parisian. Argentinians and Mexicans both speak Spanish – but can sound very different.

Telling Tales

In this unit you will be listening to tales told by a wonderful storyteller, Grace Hallworth. You will be finding out what it takes to tell a story well and you will be telling stories yourself.

you will be....

- Commenting on written texts
- Responding to a writer
- Telling a story

Grace Hallworth writes . . .

WE are all tellers of tales or story tellers. We tell stories about our dreams, our fears and our triumphs. Everyone enjoys sharing jokes, tall tales and shaggy dog stories. As we grow older, we talk about things that have happened to us a long time in the past. We may add bits and pieces here and there to make the stories more interesting!

Anyone who enjoys telling stories soon learns how to make them really enjoyable – both for the teller and the listener. It's always easiest to tell a story which you yourself like. You can then make it your own. You can take it into your inner world and tell it with real feeling. Of course, you still have to know all the details of the story so that you can make vivid pictures for your listeners. Getting to know a story you want to tell is not simply a matter of learning it off by heart. You have to pay attention to the way things happen. You have to be sure how one character relates to another, just as in a play or a film. You have to choose carefully the words you use to tell your story – you have to use words which will make the story come alive for whoever is listening to you. You have to make your words – and your story – fit your audience.

I say that when I tell a story, I 'lose myself in it'. By this I mean that I enter the story world so completely, that I feel as though I'm actually there, experiencing the events I'm telling. I never tell the same story in exactly the same way twice because, every time I tell it, I recreate a slightly different story world for myself.

As a storyteller, I draw on what I see around me and my thoughts about life. I also have to use my imagination. It is my imagination which helps me to sense the right moment to change the rhythm of the story, or the pace at which I'm speaking. A well-timed pause creates tension – what is going to happen next? I use other techniques too to help make my stories come alive for my listeners. I may give my eyes a particular expression. I may curl my lips, I may slightly tilt my head. All these gestures add to the power of the story – and so to the listeners' enjoyment of it.

When I tell a story, I like my listeners to be as close to me as possible and on the same level. This makes eye contact easier. It also helps produce a feeling that everyone is about to share something – as friends. When I tell stories, I'm not weighed down by having to read something in front of me. I am able to concentrate on my listeners. I can sense how they are responding to the drama I am unfolding. I can sometimes put into a story things which have something to do with members of my audience. This makes them feel more involved in the story. I never do so much of this, though, that I lose sight of the original tale. I try to make room in my story telling for my audience to 'take part'. This helps keep their attention focused on me and the tale. I often find that bringing in a song helps join me with my listeners. In many parts of Black Africa, singing is a central part of storytelling. There may also be mime, acting out, dance and drumming. In this way, the story telling becomes a 'performance'. This tends to happen particularly in places where there is a strong community spirit – where people share certain ideas and beliefs which are passed on by word of mouth. Such performance tellings take place at gatherings called 'ceilidhs' in some villages in Scotland and Ireland. The 'corroboree' of Australian aborigines, the 'parang' of villages in Trinidad and the 'pow-pow' of native Americans, are all occasions when people come together to celebrate. They combine story, song, dance and drumming, acting out and mime into a performance.

We are all human beings. We all share the same basic feelings – love, hope, fear, excitement. We all share the same worries – about living and dying. Traditional tales – myths, legends, folktales – often deal with these human feelings and concerns and they are the same the world over. Nevertheless, they do take on the colour, expressions, rhythms and local customs of the country where they are told. In three legends which come from France, England and Canada, the plots are almost the same, but there's a dog instead of a cat in the English legend!

Stories about mermaids and fairymaids (the female of the species) are told all over the world, in places as far away from one another as the island of Tobago in the Caribbean, and the North of Scotland. In Scotland, tales are told about the 'Selchie' who is a seal in the sea and a man or woman on the land. Fairymaids and mermaids live in the rivers and seas of the Caribbean. They, too, can live on land, but are more likely to lure human beings to their home beneath the water. In both Caribbean and Scottish folklore, the fairymaid is always extremely beautiful with, on the one hand, long black hair and, on the other, long white or golden hair. On the tape you will be listening to, I tell two mer-folk legends: *Nothing But a Pair of Shoes* comes from Tobago, *The White Seal Maid* from Scotland. Both tales deal with a relationship between a man and a fairymaid. But the *mood* of the two stories is very different and so I tell them differently. When I tell *Nothing But a Pair of Shoes*, I am describing an unusual incident in which I only half-believe. With *The White Seal Maid*, I am completely inside the story. The structure, the rhythms, the words of the story draw me into the sadness of the tale. With this story, I find it more difficult to change and recreate the story world each time. In the written version, which you have printed in your books, the sense of magic and mystery is already so powerful. But in my telling of it, I hope I bring out the rhythms and the changes in pace which lie behind the words to make the story come even more alive.

Listening to the stories

Talking about the stories

Get into groups and discuss these things:

[1] **What happened in the stories**
Were you curious to find out what happened next? Did you think you knew the ending?

[2] **The way Grace told them**
Which of the things that Grace wrote about could you imagine her doing as you listened to the story? How did she use the tone of her voice to show the feelings of the characters? How did she build up excitement? Did she pause? When? Why?

[3] **The individual stories**
Which did you like most? Why? Which 'telling' did you like most? Why? Which tale would you like to be able to retell? Which would you find easiest?

Now still in your groups, read the printed version of *The White Seal Maid* on the following two pages. Share the reading.

Tips for Success

When listening to a story . . .

- Concentrate on the story and the rhythm of the words.
- Like Grace, try hard to picture the scene in your mind.
- Sit quietly for a moment or two after the story has finished so that it stays in your mind.

The White Seal Maid

ON THE NORTH SEA shore there was a fisherman named Merdock who lived all alone. He had neither wife nor child, nor wanted one. At least that was what he told the other men with whom he fished the banks.

But truth was, Merdock was a lonely man, at ease only with the wind and waves. And each evening, when he left his companions, calling out 'Fair wind' – the sailor's leave – he knew they were going back to a warm hearth and a full bed while he went home to none. Secretly he longed for the same comfort.

One day it came to Merdock as if in a dream that he should leave off fishing that day and go down to the sea-ledge and hunt the seal. He had never done such a thing before, thinking it close to murder, for the seal had human eyes and cried with a baby's voice.

Yet though he had never done such a thing, there was such a longing within him that Merdock could not say no to it. And that longing was like a high, sweet singing, a calling. He could not rid his mind of it. So he went.

Down by a gray rock he sat, a long sharpened stick by his side. He kept his eyes fixed out on the sea, where the white birds sat on the waves like foam.

He waited through sunrise and sunset and through the long, cold night, the singing in his head. Then, when the wind went down a bit, he saw a white seal far out in the sea, coming towards him, the moon riding on its shoulder.

Merdock could scarcely breathe as he watched the seal, so shining and white was its head. It swam swiftly to the sea-ledge, and then with one quick push it was on land.

Merdock rose then in silence, the stick in his hand. He would have thrown it, too. But the white seal gave a sudden shudder and its skin sloughed off. It was a maiden cast in moonlight, with the tide about her feet.

She stepped high out of her skin, and her hair fell sleek and white about her shoulders and hid her breasts.

Merdock fell to his knees behind the rock and would have hidden his eyes, but her cold white beauty was too much for him. He could only stare. And if he made a noise then, she took no notice but turned her face to the sea and opened her arms up to the moon. Then she began to sway and call.

At first Merdock could not hear the words. Then he realised it was the very song he had heard in his head all that day:

> Come to the edge,
> Come down to the ledge
> Where the water laps the shore.
>
> Come to the strand,
> Seals to the sand,
> The watery time is o'er.

When the song was done, she began it again. It was as if the whole beach, the whole cove, the whole world were nothing but that one song.

And as she sang, the water began to fill up with seals. Black seals and gray seals and seals of every kind. They swam to the shore at her call and sloughed off their skins. They were as young as the white seal maid, but none so beautiful in Merdock's eyes. They swayed and turned at her singing, and joined their voices to hers. Faster and faster the seal maidens danced, in circles of twos and threes and fours. Only the white seal maid danced alone, in the center, surrounded by the cast off skins of her twirling sisters.

The moon remained high almost all the night, but at last it went down. At its setting, the seal maids stopped their singing, put on their skins again, one by one, went back into the sea again, one by one, and swam away. But the white seal maid did not go. She waited on the shore until the last of them was out of sight.

Then she turned to the watching man, as if she had always known he was there, hidden behind the gray rock. There was something strange, a kind of pleading, in her eyes.

Merdock read that pleading and thought he understood it. He ran over to where she stood, grabbed up her sealskin, and held it high overhead.

'Now you be mine,' he said.

And she had to go with him, that was the way of it. For she was a selchie, one of the seal folk. And the old tales said it: The selchie maid without her skin was no more than a lass.

They were wed within the week, Merdock and the white seal maid, because he wanted it. So she nodded her head at the priest's bidding, though she said not a word.

And Merdock had no complaint of her, his 'Sel' as he called her. No complaint except this: she would not go down to the sea. She would not go down by the shore where he had found her or down to the sand to see him in his boat, though often enough she would stare from the cottage door out past the cove's end where the inlet poured out into the great wide sea.

'Will you not walk down by the water's edge with me, Sel?' Merdock would ask each morning. 'Or will you not come down to greet me when I return?'

She never answered him, either 'Yea' or 'Nay.' Indeed, if he had not heard her singing that night on the ledge, he would have thought her mute. But she was a good wife, for all that, and did what he required. If she did not smile, she did not weep. She seemed, to Merdock, strangely content.

So Merdock hung the white sealskin up over the door where Sel could see it. He kept it there in case she should want to leave him, to don the skin and go. He could have hidden it or burned it, but he did not. He hoped the sight of it, so near and easy, would keep her with him; would tell her, as he could not, how much he loved her. For he found he did love her, his seal wife. It was that simple. He loved her and did not want her to go, but he would not keep her past her willing it, so he hung the skin up over the door.

And then their sons were born. One a year, born at the ebbing of the tide. And Sel sang to them, one by one, long, longing wordless songs that carried the sound of the sea. But to Merdock she said nothing.

Seven sons they were, strong and silent, one born each year. They were born to the sea, born to swim, born to let the tide lap them head and shoulder. And though they had the dark eyes of the seal, and though they had the seal's longing for the sea, they were men and had men's names: James, John, Michael, George, William, Rob, and Tom. They helped their father fish the cove and bring home his catch from the sea.

It was seven years and seven years and seven years again that the seal wife lived with him. The oldest of their sons was just coming to his twenty-first birthday, the youngest barely a man. It was on a gray day, the wind scarcely rising, that the boys all refused to go with Merdock when he called. They gave no reason but 'Nay.'

'Wife,' Merdock called, his voice heavy and gray as the sky. 'Wife, whose sons are these? How have you raised them that they say "Nay" to their father when he calls?' It was ever his custom to talk to Sel as if she returned him words.

To his surprise, Sel turned to him and said, 'Go. My sons be staying with me this day.' It was the voice of the singer on the beach, musical and low. And the shock was so great that he went at once and did not look back.

He set his boat on the sea, the great boat that usually took several men to row it. He set it out himself, and got it out into the cove, put the nets over, and never once heard when his sons called out to him as he went, 'Father, fair wind!'

But after a bit the shock wore thin and he began to think about it. He became angry then, at his sons and at his wife, who had long plagued him with her silence. He pulled in the nets and pulled on the oars and started toward home. 'I, too, can say "Nay" to this sea,' he said out loud as he rode the swells in.

The beach was cold and empty. Even the gulls were mute.

'I do not like this,' Merdock said. 'It smells of a storm.'

He beached the boat and walked home. The sky gathered in around him. At the cottage he hesitated but a moment, then pulled savagely on the door. He waited for the warmth to greet him. But the house was as empty and cold as the beach.

Merdock went into the house and stared at the hearth, black and silent. Then, fear riding in his heart, he turned slowly and looked over the door.

The sealskin was gone.

'Sel!' he cried then as he ran from the house, and he named his sons in a great anguished cry as he ran. Down to the sea-ledge he went, calling their names like a prayer: 'James, John, Michael, George, William, Rob, Tom!'

But they were gone.

The rocks were gray, as gray as the sky. At the water's edge was a pile of clothes that lay like discarded skins. Merdock stared out far across the cove and saw a seal herd swimming. Yet not a herd. A white seal and seven strong pups.

'Sel!' he cried again. 'James, John, Michael, George, William, Rob, Tom!'

For a moment, the white seal turned her head, then she looked again to the open sea and barked out seven times. The wind carried the faint sounds back to the shore. Merdock heard, as if in a dream, the seven seal names she called. They seemed harsh and jangling to his ear.

Then the whole herd dived. When they came up again they were but eight dots strung along the horizon, lingering for a moment, then disappearing into the blue edge of sea.

Merdock recited the seven seal names to himself. And in that recitation was a song, a litany to the god of the seals. The names were no longer harsh, but right. And he remembered clearly again the moonlit night when the seals had danced upon the sand. Maidens all. Not a man or boy with them. And the white seal turning and choosing him, giving herself to him that he might give the seal people life.

His anger and sadness left him then. He turned once more to look at the sea and pictured his seven strong sons on their way.

He shouted their seal names to the wind. Then he added, under his breath, as if trying out a new tongue, 'Fair wind, my sons. Fair wind.'

◆ ◆

Compare the written story and the told story . . .

1. Did Grace leave out anything when she told the story? Why do you think she might have done this?

2. Did Grace add anything? Why do you think she might have done this?

3. Which did you find more moving – the written story or the told story? Why?

Telling Your Tale

Now it's your turn to tell a story. This is a tale which comes from the Caribbean.

FIRST . . .

1 Get into pairs. Read *Never Play With Fire* together aloud.

Never Play with Fire

A young man was walking along a road one night bemoaning his bad fortune.

'O life!' he cried. 'So this is what you bring me to. You rob me of house and home, you rob me of friends and I don't even have a place to lay my head. O life! I would give my soul for a crust of bread.'

Just then he saw a figure coming towards him. As it drew near, the young man made out a very tall man with eyes that seemed to smoulder in the dark. He was elegantly dressed in a frilled white shirt and a well-tailored suit. When he spoke his voice was as smooth as butter.

'I could not help but overhear your words. Truly life has not been kind to you. Even so you must be in a bad state to make so rash an offer,' the tall man said.

'Sir, nothing could be worse than what I have suffered these last three years. Not even the loss of a soul,' replied the young man.

Still the stranger pressed, 'Do you mean that you would exchange a soul for bread and bed?'

His taunting manner annoyed the young man. 'Look at me, man! Look at the condition of my bare feet! Look at the rags I wear! That is what people judge me by when I ask for a job, a piece of bread, or a bed for the night. Yes, I can do without a soul.'

'Good,' said the stranger. 'Since you are so sure, I will make a bargain with you. I will give you the opportunity to become successful but one day I shall return for the payment of a soul. Is it a deal?'

Well, anyone with a grain of sense would have backed down, said some 'Hail Marys,' or taken to his heels but the young man was desperate and decided to brazen it out. He agreed. The following morning he came to his senses but it was too late. The contract was sealed and stamped. The stranger had vanished.

Time passed and the young man forgot all about the incident. He found a job as an assistant manager on a large cocoa estate and a year later, when the manager died in a mysterious way, he was promoted. And a good manager he was too, for the estate flourished. The family who owned the estate became more and more dependent on the young man's advice and their generosity knew no bounds. Only one thing was lacking to make his happiness complete.

His employers had an only child, a beautiful and modest daughter. The young man had fallen deeply in love with her and he knew she was fond of him. Yet he held back from telling her how he felt.

One day the girl's father took him aside and said, 'My boy, have you ever thought of getting married?'

The question was so sudden that the young man was at a loss for words. He had to play for time until he knew which way the wind was blowing.

'Sir,' he replied. 'You know that marriage got teeth and

need much thought and time. All my thoughts are on the estate and I have no time to think about a wife.'

The father was pleased with the young man's reply. True, he had not heard the young man's name linked with any of the local girls but he had to make sure.

'Well, then,' said the father. 'Let me make you a proposition. Would you consider marriage with my daughter? I believe she is fond of you and the estate will be in good hands when I am dead and gone.'

The young man was beside himself with joy and lost no time in proposing to the girl. She accepted the offer of marriage willingly and soon preparations for the wedding were in full swing. The young man spent most of his spare time designing and building fittings and furniture for the new house which the girl's parents had given them as a wedding present. He was an excellent craftsman and put his heart and soul into making things which were beautiful as well as useful. But now his luck took a bad turn.

One evening he was working late on a piece of furniture when suddenly he felt so cold that his hands were seized with cramp and he could not hold the tools. He shivered and as he went to close the open door he saw a man framed in the doorway.

'I see that you are doing well, very well indeed,' said a voice which stirred a memory. 'Now it is time for payment and the keeping of a promise.'

'Who are you?' enquired the young man peering at the stranger's face which was hidden in shadow.

'I met you five years ago poor, hungry and in rags and offered you all that you have now,' said the visitor coming into the room so that the young man could see his face.

There was no need to do so for the young man had suddenly remembered that hypnotic voice which had tempted him to make a rash deal, a deal which might now cost him more than life. Every limb of his body trembled at the thought of it, but the same fear that made him shake as if in a fever, sharpened his wits.

'You are a fair-minded man,' he said. 'So let me first set everything in order with my employer and I will pay you what I owe.'

'Very well,' said the man. 'I will give you seven days and then I shall return to hold you to your bargain.'

The young man could not sleep that night for thinking how he might save his soul. And he was tortured with visions of indescribable horror. He moaned and tossed and wept, 'Ay-a-ay! To have come so near to Paradise only to be dragged deep into Hell.'

Early next morning he set out to see an old Spanish woman who lived at the top of the mountain. He told her about his meeting with the tall man who had promised him all he desired and had now returned to take his soul.

'Man, when you play with fire you must expect to get burn,' she said. 'It is El Diablo himself you gambling your life with and maybe I can help or maybe I cannot. I will do what I can.'

She gave him a special prayer to repeat seven times a day for seven days of waiting. She gave him a crucifix to wear around his neck. Last of all she gave him something wrapped in a black cloth which she placed in a small wooden box. 'You must see no one for the seven days and no food must pass your lips but water. When the devil comes, give him the box. He alone must open it and until he does you will not know what is inside.'

When the young man left the old woman he went directly to his employer and asked for one week's leave to attend to important business. Then he returned home, locked his door and began his vigil. On the seventh day he awoke early and placed the box on the table near him. The day passed slowly and night came. Not a cricket chirped and the nightly chorus of frogs was hushed.

A few minutes after midnight there was a strong gust of wind which broke the door off its hinges and sent it crashing to the floor. At the same time the lights flickered and went out leaving the place in darkness. The young man did not move from his seat near the table, but his hands tightened around the box which the old woman had given him. He waited.

The room was lit up by a figure outlined by a circle of flames. The strong stench of sulphur filled the young man's nostrils; his attention was held by a pair of eyes which burned into his head destroying his will. Silently he began to recite the prayer that the old woman had given him and soon there was no fire in his head. A voice spoke, 'I have come to complete our bargain.' The young man handed him the box without a word.

'Why do you give me this?' asked the voice. The young man remained silent.

The stranger opened the box and unwrapped the cloth. His sharp intake of breath sounded like the hiss of a viper before it strikes its victim.

'How dare you mock me?' he asked and the venom in his soft voice sent a chill through the young man, who in turn looked at the contents of the box. All hope left him. He had been so sure that the old woman had given him some holy relic which would terrify the evil one and send him scuttling back to Hell. Instead she had placed the SOLE of a shoe in the box!

The words went round and round in his brain 'THE SOLE OF A SHOE! THE SOLE OF A SHOE FOR HIS SOUL!' Then he heard himself speaking words which seemed to come from outside him, 'It is true that we made a deal,' he said. 'But you never spelt out exactly what you wanted of me and you will agree that the word has many meanings. Why, it might be the underside of my foot, or again, it might be a fish. And surely it could also be part of a plough, or even . . .' He never finished the list of what the word might have meant. The devil (for he it was) threw down the box and its contents on the floor and disappeared into a bright yellow flame which floated through the door, and was gone.

The young man breathed deeply for the first time in seven days. Then he wept a little from sheer relief, and who could blame him? He had gone through a terrible ordeal – one which he would never forget as long as he lived. As for the sole of the shoe, he wrapped it in the black cloth and stored it safely in the box to remind him of his narrow escape. And if you look at the sole carefully you can still see the scorch marks where the devil held it.

NEXT . . .

2 Read the story again and think about:

- **The tone of your voice**
  What tone of voice are you going to use for the different characters? There are plenty of clues in the story. For example, you are told that the stranger's voice is 'as smooth as butter' and that the young man is 'bemoaning his bad fortune'. How can you show this smoothness and this moaning tone when you tell the story?

- **The pace of your telling**
  Where will you vary the speed of your telling? Which bits will have to be slow and relaxed. Which will have to be fast, exciting or furious? Where should you pause and look at your audience?

3 Without looking at your book, try a first telling to your partner, or you could tell the story together. Don't worry about bits you forget. Just do your best to tell the story so that what you say makes sense.

If you find this difficult, jot down a few notes about the events and the names of the characters.

Listen carefully to your partner. What is he or she doing right? Where is the telling sounding dull?

Are there gaps in your story? Are there things which you need to explain? Often, when you go from a written story to a told one, it helps to put in more of the words actually spoken by people. For example, when you tell of the young man's visit to the Spanish woman you could make up the words of the prayer she told him to repeat.

4 Look at the written story again at this stage, if you feel you need to. Don't worry if your version is rather different. It could be just as good – or better!

FINALLY . . .

5 Tell the story again to your partner or to a small group. As you listen to other tellers, see what they do well. Try to decide what are the *three* most important things you must do when telling a story. You might want to look back at what Grace says about this, too.

Tips for Success

When telling a story . . .

- Keep the beginning, middle and end of the story clearly in your head.
- Sit close to your listeners and look at them.
- Vary the pace of the story. Pause sometimes and add excitement. Speak loudly enough for your audience to hear.
- Use gestures sometimes if you find these help.
- Make your characters come alive by the way in which you make them speak.

That reminds me!

This unit will help you to think hard about things which have happened to you. It will show you how to develop these past experiences into poems and stories. In this unit you will also have the chance to discover how Gareth Owen, a professional writer, makes use of both his imagination and his *memory* when he writes.

When you read a poem or a book, or watch a film or a play, it is easy to forget that it was written by a writer who sat down in front of a blank sheet of paper and thought about what to write. The ideas that end up as your reading or viewing came from inside that writer and from his or her experiences of the real world.

You might like to read through the poems below. What past event sparked off each poem?

you will be....

Responding to a writer

Relating personal experience

GRANNY GRANNY
PLEASE COMB MY HAIR

Granny Granny
please comb my hair
you always take your time
you always take such care

You put me to sit on a cushion
between your knees
you rub a little coconut oil
parting gentle as a breeze

Mummy Mummy
she's always in a hurry – hurry
rush
she pulls my hair
sometimes she tugs

But Granny
you have all the time in the world
and when you're finished
you always turn my head and say
'Now who's a nice girl.'

Grace Nichols

DEAD DOG

One day I found a lost dog in the street.
The hairs about its jaw were spiked with blood,
And it lay still as stone. It must have been
A little dog,
For though I only stood
Nine inches for each one of my four years
I picked it up and took it home. My mother
Squealed, and later father spaded out
A bed and tucked my mongrel down in mud.

I can't remember any feeling but
A moderate pity, cool not swollen-eyed;
Almost a god-like feeling now it seems.
My lump of dog was ordinary as bread.
I have no recollection of the school
Where I was taught my terror of the dead.

Vernon Scannell

Memory chaining

Have you ever wondered what happens to memories of the experiences you've had in your life? They are stored away, mysteriously, in your brain and often surface unexpectedly when you are day-dreaming, reading, or talking to somebody.

It is possible to work at bringing them back. You can then select from these memories to write a poem or story for other people to read.

You will know from the List Poems unit, that words have associations – they make you think of other words and ideas.

Memory chaining works in a similar way. It gets you to write one memory down – this will in turn remind you of another memory and so on. Each memory you think of is like a link in a chain which helps to build up a picture. That's why the technique is called 'memory chaining'.

Now follow these steps:

1. Head the left-hand page of your notebook 'Memory writing'. Spend 10–15 minutes writing down a memory chain about a particular time in your life. List the memories briefly, using a short phrase or a single sentence at most. Aim to list as many memories as you can. Don't go for too much detail at this stage.

2. Now head the right-hand page of your notebook 'Comments'. Write down here which memories seem most interesting to you and why. Which memories were ones you thought you had forgotten about?

3. Your memory chain could give you enough material to keep you writing for months. But, for the moment, just choose one of the memories which you feel you want to develop further. If you can't decide for yourself, show your memory chain and comments to someone else and ask them to say which memory they'd like to read more about.

MEMORY WRITING

On holiday near Bournemouth 1985

When that dog bit me

It was in a thunder storm

Simon ran off and left me

He was supposed to take me to the shops!!!

I dropped my sweets

I cried a lot

Simon got into big trouble

Never saw the dog again though

COMMENTS

We went there every year – it was a bungalow made out of an old railway carriage

The sky was black – you couldn't see where it joined the sea.

– my brother!

We used to buy Blackjacks – little black liquorice toffee in squares – they made your tongue go black

I suppose it was the shock really – maybe I wanted to get him into trouble.

It didn't rain again either!

I remember the year my little sister Carol was born.

I had the day off school to visit my mother in hospital.

When she was 9 months old Carol fell down the stairs

I spent the Easter holidays with my uncle and aunt in the country

I saw a lamb being born

My pet gerbil died while I was away

we moved house

The neighbours' house was broken in to.

At my birthday party, everyone dressed up as ghosts

I was given a new stamp album by my aunt

I was given another new stamp album by another aunt

I broke my mother's favourite vase

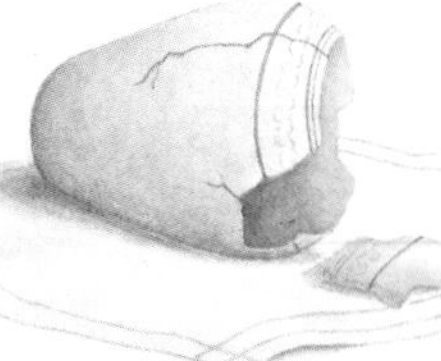

Sometimes, getting started on memory chains is a problem. It may help if you use a 'hook' to start your ideas off. You could think of one particular summer holiday, one particular year (e.g. the year you started infant school or the year a younger brother or sister was born).

Or you could start off your memory chain using phrases like, 'My earliest memories are . . .', 'My most painful memories are . . .', 'My favourite memories are . . .'. Starters like these will help you to get going.

Tight focusing

[4] You are now going to write a lot more about your chosen memory. You will need to add more detail about events, places, people, feelings.

To help you remember this detail, you are going to use another technique called 'tight focusing'.

Get into pairs. You now have to ask one another more and more detailed questions about your chosen memory. The example below shows the sort of questions you would ask someone who was trying to remember as much as possible about 'the day we moved house'.

ONE

What time of year was it? What day of the week was it? What sort of house or flat were you moving from? What sort of house or flat were you moving to?

TWO

Focus in . . .

What time did the removal men arrive? How many of them were there? Which room did they start clearing first? What were your parents doing while the rooms were being cleared?

THREE

Focus in closer . . .

What were the men wearing? How many cups of tea did they drink? How many men did it take to carry the sofa? Did anything get broken? What?

FOUR

Focus in still closer . . .

What was the boss called? What colour was his hair? What did he say to your parents when he arrived? What was the last thing left hanging on the wall of your room? What was your last thought as you walked out of the front door?

[5] Before you work your chosen memory into a finished piece of writing, you need to ask yourself these questions:

- Do I want to write a poem or a story?
- What effect do I want to have on my readers? Do I want to amuse them? Surprise them? Frighten them?

You are now thinking about your reader and writing for an audience. This is an important stage in becoming a good writer.

[6] Write a first draft of your poem or story. Then try this out on a partner if you like, to see what he or she thinks of it. Redraft it if necessary. You may need to make cuts if it's too long and boring. You may need to add detail if something important isn't described fully enough.

A Day in the Country

That summer Saturday they took us by coach
deep into the countryside, a sixty-mile journey,
told us how much we should enjoy it,
forty of us and four of our teachers.

Once off the motorway we were soon there,
a village with a tall spired church,
one street, thatched houses dotted here and there,
a public house and a shop where they sold
everything from stamps to pet food and bacon;
we bought ice creams there.

We ate our sandwiches on the vicar's lawn,
he gave us lemonade and strawberries,
and said we could go anywhere
but must shut all gates behind us.
I went with my teacher to the church,
marble monuments and flowers,
a Saxon font, box pews and a musty smell,
wandered around the overgrown graveyard,
reading the names and the dates on the tombs.

Then we all walked by the river,
saw some men and a heron fishing,
cows standing in the cool waters;
back through long fields of sheep
and a little wood loud with birds.

We played games in a daisied meadow,
got stung by wasps, chased by a bull,
and spoke to a farmer
who was just about to start milking.
But there was nothing to do,
I was bored with it all.

Before we left, some white-haired old ladies
gave us tea in a flowery garden,
bread and butter, milk and rock cakes,
asked us our names.

At last we crowded into the coach,
sang all the way home.

How glad we were to get back
to our noisy streets, to the shops we knew,
football, cinemas, the telly,
riding our bikes on the pavement,
fish and chips, Coca-Cola,
our homes towering into the sky,
father and mother coming in from work,
our friends of every colour.

They were kind to us in the village,
good to lie in the sun,
but one day was enough.
I should not like to live there,
everybody was so old,
and there were only six children.

Leonard Clark

Now meet Gareth Owen

Gareth Owen has written two novels and three books of poems for young people.

SALFORD ROAD
Poems
By
GARETH OWEN
'Vividly recaptures the joys and sorrows of childhood.'

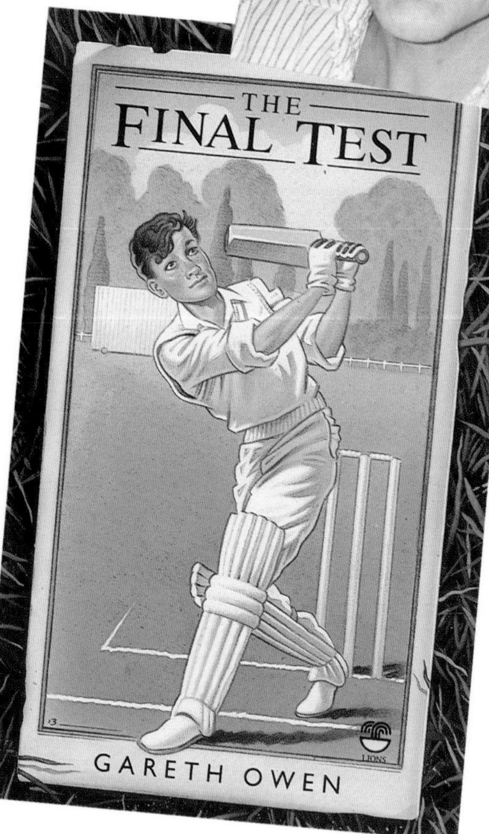

‘ I will sometimes use real place and street names in my books. I don't suppose it matters to the reader but it seems to make the story more real for me. When I sit down to write, I usually start with an event that actually took place, it seems to help me. It makes it easier for me to invent other events which I can put around it. In the final version, the original idea may be left out altogether. ’

‘ Some poems are quite close to the truth. *My Sister Betty*, for example. When I was eight and my sister about twelve she used to come into my bedroom and die theatrically every night on the lino. I suppose when I was writing the poem I was thinking, too, of my bedroom and the geography of our house. None of that comes into the poem but it's still important for me to think about things like this when I am writing. It allows me to sink myself into the poem. I would say that I've never written a poem or story where I haven't gone back into myself. ’

‘ I suppose everything I write is autobiographical in some way. But very few of my poems and stories actually deal with events that have happened to me. In many of them I pretend to be someone else. I try to take on his or her character and voice. In a way, it's acting with a pen. ’

SALFORD ROAD

Salford Road, Salford Road,
This is the place where I was born,
With a green front gate, a red brick wall
And hydrangeas round a lawn.

Salford Road, Salford Road,
Is the road where we would play
Where the sky lay over the roof tops
Like a friend who'd come to stay.

The Gardeners lived at fifty-five,
The Lunds with the willow tree,
Mr Pool with the flag and the garden pond
And the Harndens at fifty-three.

There was riding bikes and laughing
Till we couldn't laugh any more,
And bilberries picked on the hillside
And picnics on the shore.

I lay in bed when I was four
As the sunlight turned to grey
And heard the train through my pillow
And the seagulls far away.

And I rose to look out of my window
For I knew that someone was there
And a man stood as sad as nevermore
And didn't see me there.

And when I stand in Salford Road
And think of the boy who was me
I feel that from one of the windows
Someone is looking at me.

My friends walked out one Summer day,
Walked singing down the lane,
My friends walked into a wood called Time
And never came out again.

We live in a land called Gone-Today
That's made of bricks and straw
But Salford Road runs through my head
To a land called Evermore.

My Sister Betty

My sister Betty said,
'I'm going to be a famous actress.'
Last year she was going to be a missionary.
'Famous actresses always look unhappy but beautiful,'
She said, pulling her mouth sideways
And making her eyes turn upwards
So they were mostly white.
'Do I look unhappy but beautiful?'
'I want to go to bed and read,' I said.
'Famous actresses suffer and have hysterics,' she said.
'I've been practising my hysterics.'
She began going very red and screaming
So that it hurt my ears.
She hit herself on the head with her fists
And rolled off my bed on to the lino.
I stood by the wardrobe where it was safer.
She got up saying, 'Thank you, thank you,'
And bowed to the four corners of my bedroom.
'Would you like an encore of hysterics?' she asked.
'No,' I said from inside the wardrobe.
There was fluff all over her vest.
'If you don't clap enthusiastically,' she said,
'I'll put your light out when you're reading.'
While I clapped a bit
She bowed and shouted, 'More, more!'
Auntie Gladys shouted upstairs,
'Go to bed and stop teasing our Betty.'
'The best thing about being a famous actress,' Betty said,
'Is that you get to die a lot.'
She fell to the floor with a crash
And lay there for an hour and a half
With her eyes staring at the ceiling.
She only went away when I said,
'You really look like a famous actress
Who's unhappy but beautiful.'

When I got into bed and started reading,
She came and switched off my light.
It's not much fun
Having a famous actress for a sister.

Memory Storming with Gareth Owen

'Everything that has ever happened to a writer is stored somewhere, waiting to be set in its place in a story when needed.

Memory storming sessions like the one you are going to listen to are the best way I've found of trying to show how stories are written. What happens during a memory storming session is this. The children and I sit down together at a table on which there is a big piece of paper. The idea is that everything which will form the backbone of the story comes from *them*. My job is to ask them the kind of questions I normally ask my own memory and imagination when I set about writing a story. I make rough notes of what the children tell me. I then select from the information, turning the raw material into a story. The whole session takes about an hour.'

First listen to the session and then read the story.

MY ACTING CAREER

It was the egg, the zebra and the taxi that made me give up wanting to become an actor. Perhaps I should have known from my earliest experiences that acting was not for me.

When I was four, my older sister used to make me dress up as the Queen so that she could do interviews with me. I wore a frilly paper hat and a blouse of my mum's that nearly reached my high-heeled sandals. She'd poke a microphone under my nose and ask me stupid questions:

'What's it like living in a palace your majesty?'

and

'How many princesses have you got your majesty?'

What was a four-year-old boy supposed to know about princesses and palaces? It used to end up with me running round the house with her chasing after me. Once I fell off my high heels and twisted my ankle. Years later I still walk with a bit of a limp.

Later there were other plays. Shopping was very popular for a time. She'd lay out a counter in the garage and cover it in boxes that were supposed to be fruit and vegetables. I had to come in and buy something. It was better than dressing up as the Queen but nobody could call it exciting.

My next role was trouble-shooter for the Gas Board. She'd pretend to ring me up and ask me to go round and fix her gas cooker. I had to wear this stupid peaked cap that was about three sizes too big and drink endless cups of imaginary tea while she rattled on about the weather and the cost of baby clothes. I thought if that was acting they could keep it. What I wanted was danger, excitement, blood and violence. Drinking tea was something I could do in my real life.

When I was seven, things started to look up. Tarzan came into our lives. I don't know who had the idea first but I had to dress up in a piece of imitation leopard skin that belonged to my mum and rescue my sister from an alligator that was threatening to eat her in the paddling pool. I loved that. The alligator was our poodle. I'd tie him to the paddling pool and then drop, yodelling, on top of him from a big oak tree. I don't know what the poodle thought about it but I loved it.

What really put me off acting for good, though, was when we did 'The Golden Goose' at school in front of all the parents. I wanted to be the poor woodcutter who makes the princess laugh but Mrs Speak said I had to be a peasant. It was really boring. I had hardly anything to say and had to march up and down along with ten other people carrying a spear and singing a song.

The big moment of the play was when Ann-Marie Jarraud, who was playing the goose, laid an enormous golden egg. She didn't really lay it of course. It had been hidden in the big nest by Mrs Speak before the play started. Then the goose was supposed to dance round the nest flapping her wings until the prince noticed the egg. Then she would waddle in a circle flapping her wings and quacking while everybody sang a song about the egg. It was the climax of the play.

Anyway, when the moment arrived I could tell just by looking at the goose that something had gone wrong. She started gazing round and forgot to cluck. Then the prince said his line, 'Oh my wonderful goose look at the precious, golden egg you've laid for me.' But there wasn't an egg in sight. The prince and the goose just stood there, shuffling their feet. Then they looked across towards Mrs Speak and shrugged their shoulders. The prince started giggling.

Mrs Speak hit her forehead with her hand.

'The egg,' she said, 'I forgot the egg.'

She turned to me. 'Go and fetch it quick.'

I started off round the back of the stage, and then remembered.

'Where is it Miss?'

'Room 8. Quick!'

All the classes were empty. Outside the sky was dark and it started to rain. The lights were on in the corridor. In our school, there's a door across the main corridor that divides the upper from the lower school. Usually it's kept open but on this day it had been locked to keep the noise out. I squinted through the glass. I could see the egg on Mrs Speak's desk, huge and gleaming and golden. But I couldn't get to it. In order to reach Room 8 I had to run out into the playground, down the main road and then in through the main entrance in Linaker Street. As I ran, I thought about the goose and the prince hanging about on stage not knowing what to do.

The egg was so big I needed both arms to carry it. I could hardly see over the top. Ann-Marie Jarraud was only little. Even with her goose costume on I couldn't imagine her laying an egg that size. I ran through the rain with it cradled in my arms like a big, round, golden baby.

Just by the zebra-crossing, my foot slipped and the egg flew out of my arms and rolled and bounced down the street. A taxi came round the corner. I saw an amazed look on the taxi driver's face as he saw a golden egg the size of a wheelbarrow flying towards him. He stamped on the brakes and the taxi skidded to a stop. But it was too late. Both wheels ran over the egg. I couldn't believe it.

The driver got out looking pale and worried. He thought he'd killed something but he didn't know what.

'What was that?' he asked.

I was really mad. I'd run miles to fetch that egg. I was covered in mud, I was soaking wet and my knee was bleeding.

'It's our egg,' I shouted. 'You ran over our egg.'

He looked at me in amazement. His mouth formed the word 'egg' but no sound came out. A lady passenger in high heels got out of the taxi.

'What's the matter?' she asked.

'We ran over an egg,' said the taxi driver.

I climbed to my feet out of the gutter. 'It wasn't an ordinary egg. It was a golden egg,' I shouted.

The lady raised her eyebrows. 'Oh, I see,' she said and got back into the taxi.

I walked over towards the egg. It was lying in the gutter. It was flat and caked with mud. There were black marks where the tyres had run over it. It didn't look much like an egg any more. I picked it up carefully as if it was an injured dog and walked slowly across the playground through the rain.

I came to the hall windows where the play was being acted and peeped through. The audience were talking amongst themselves. The goose and the prince were sitting on a hay bale. They looked as if they were waiting for a train to arrive. Mrs Speak was walking up and down looking at the floor and running her fingers through her hair.

I looked down at the broken, flattened remains of the egg. There didn't seem much sense in Anne-Marie laying a piece of cardboard. I threw it on to the ground. The rain fell on it.

The taxi was coming round the corner. The driver was smoking a cigarette and smiling. I could hear the music from his car radio. He seemed to have got over the shock of the accident. I thought it must be warm and dry in the cab. I gave a last look through the rain-streaked window at the play. I put my hands in my pockets, shuffled between the puddles and out into the road. Taxi driving looked a nice sort of job, I thought.

Follow-up ideas

Work in pairs

[1] Think back to the memory storming session you listened to.

— Write down a list of all the incidents in the story which Gareth Owen lifted straight from the information the children gave him. Here's an example to start you off: The egg was left in Room 8.

— Write down another list of things which he changed. Say why you think he made the changes.

— Write a third list of things he added. Why do you think he added these things?

[2] Read carefully what Gareth Owen says about *My Acting Career*. Then write down *five* important pieces of advice he gives about writing a story.

Compare your list with those drawn up by other pairs.

Gareth Owen talks about the story he wrote

‘*My Acting Career* is written in the first person and in the past tense. That is, it's written from the point of view of the boy using 'I', and as though the events happened some time ago.

The first person is a useful way to write. You can describe the events almost as though you were speaking. Everybody can speak and tell a story in this way and give it some style.

The sentences are very simple. For example, 'I threw it on the ground. The rain fell on it.'

Writing simply may look easy, but it isn't. I try to say one thing in each sentence and say it as clearly as possible. If you make the language complicated and fancy it can become a curtain between the reader and the events in the story. There may be pretty patterns on the curtain but you won't be able to see what is happening through the window.

Notice too that I go straight from movement, excitement and conversation to describing the weather. I jump straight from one to the other.

> '"Where is it Miss?"
> "Room 8. Quick!"
> All the classes were empty. Outside the sky was dark and it started to rain.'

I don't put this description in just for effect. The fact that it's raining is necessary to the story. It's much better to mention the fact this early in the story rather than just before he falls because it sounds more natural.

I try not to say what the characters are feeling. I don't use words like 'sad' or 'frightened' or 'bewildered' unless I have to. I give the evidence. I describe what a character *does*. I leave the readers to draw their own conclusions as to what that character is feeling. You have to leave something for the reader to do. Try not to describe feelings. Try to picture the scene and to describe it as accurately and briefly as possible. In a story, it's your job to put down action and speech. Leave the rest to the reader.

For example, I don't say that Mrs Speak is in a desperate panic. I merely describe what she does so the reader can see her. That's what you have to do: make the reader see and hear.

> 'Mrs Speak hit her forehead with her hand.
> "The egg," she said. "I forgot the egg."'

And later:

'Mrs Speak was walking up and down looking at the floor and running her fingers through her hair.'

It's important to have a good opening sentence for your story. It's got to draw people straight into the story and make them want to read it. Of course my first sentence is a bit of a cheat. There isn't a zebra in the story at all. It's a zebra crossing. But that doesn't matter. The first sentence will make people wonder what an egg, a zebra and a taxi have to do with one another. They won't know that I've cheated with the zebra until they've finished reading the story!

It's OK to write the title after you've finished the story because quite often you won't know what the story's really about until *after* you've finished writing it.

This story is supposed to be quite funny but it's real and serious as well. The funnier the story the more flatly you should write it. Be a straightfaced comedian. There's nothing worse than somebody telling you a joke and laughing all the time saying, 'Listen, this is funny.' The same goes for a story. Write it as if it's serious.

Have you noticed how much I left out? You don't even know the name of the boy or what he looks like. You don't know how old the sister is or what she looks like. The boy's mother and father don't come into it. What you leave out is as important as what you put in. I wanted the story to travel swiftly. It runs from when the boy is four until when he's eleven in two pages. That's quite a long time. I didn't have room to put in unnecessary details. I wanted to get on to the golden goose part as quickly as possible but it couldn't stand on its own.

When you're starting to write, just put down as accurately and simply as you can what you can see and hear. If you don't learn to describe what's in front of your eyes you'll never learn to describe what isn't.'

Work in small groups

3 Gareth Owen's memory storming session was all about school plays and play-acting. His story took these ideas and developed them. In your group, try to decide on a good theme to start off a memory storming session. It could be an accident that happened to you. Or the worst summer holiday you ever spent.

Carry out the session, writing down notes on a large sheet of paper. Then *each* work the notes into a story. Compare stories and read out the best one from each group to the rest of the class.

Tips for Success

- Think hard. Really concentrate when you are asked to remember.
- Listen to others. Use their ideas to help you remember more.
- Keep adding detail to your memories.
- Think about the person who is going to read your story or poem.

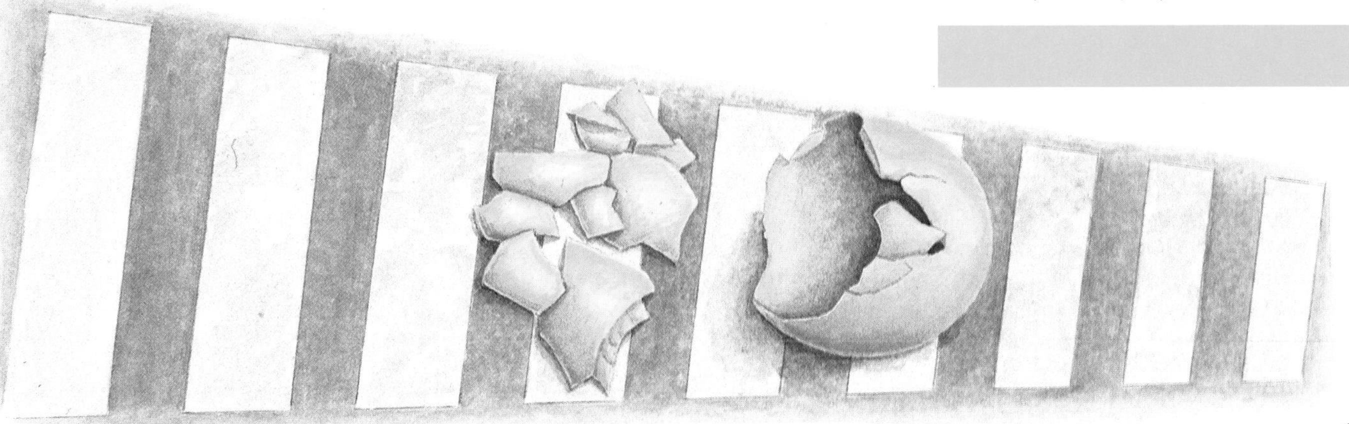

Words that sell

Advertisements use pictures and words to sell things. Slogans like 'P-P-P-Pick up a Penguin' are often clever and funny. People remember them. In this unit you will be reading about how slogans are thought up and how they help 'sell'. At the end of the unit, you will have a chance to make up slogans of your own.

Steve Smith is an advertising copywriter. It is his job to write the words for advertisements which appear on television or radio, on posters and in newspapers and magazines.

As a class or in groups, read through carefully what he says. Warning! At the end he will be asking you to do something. You'll only be able to do it well if you really concentrate on what he says.

you will be....

- **Responding to a writer**
- **Presenting information**

"If you had a cassette player and you wanted to sell it to somebody, how would you do it? You'd probably play a tape on it so they could see how well it worked.

And if you had, say, a chocolate bar, you'd let them taste a bit and hope they liked it enough to then buy a whole bar.

That's all very well if you only want to sell cassette players or chocolate bars to a few people. The trouble is, there are 55 million people in this country and the companies who want to sell things can't go around and talk to them all. Instead, they talk to them through advertising: TV and radio commercials, posters in the street, adverts in newspapers and magazines. This is very expensive. For example, it might cost £100,000 for *one* 30 second television commercial if it was shown in the middle of a really popular programme like *Coronation Street* because so many people would be watching. The longer the commercial and the more times it is shown on TV, the more it costs.

On the whole, people are more interested in watching the programmes on TV than the adverts. During the commercial break in the middle of *Coronation Street*, the amount of electricity being used in Britain goes up by half because millions of people are nipping out to the kitchen to turn on the electric kettle for a cup of tea. So a television commercial has to try to sell the product to you quickly, clearly and in such a way that it sticks in your mind. You might only see the commercial a couple of times and you might not really be paying attention when you do see it.

The pictures used in a commercial or poster are what first attract your attention. But the bit that the people doing the advertising really want you to remember is the *name* of the product and the few words of "sell" that go with it. If the commercial doesn't make you remember the name of the product it's a waste of money.

Electricity consumption during the transmission of *Coronation Street*

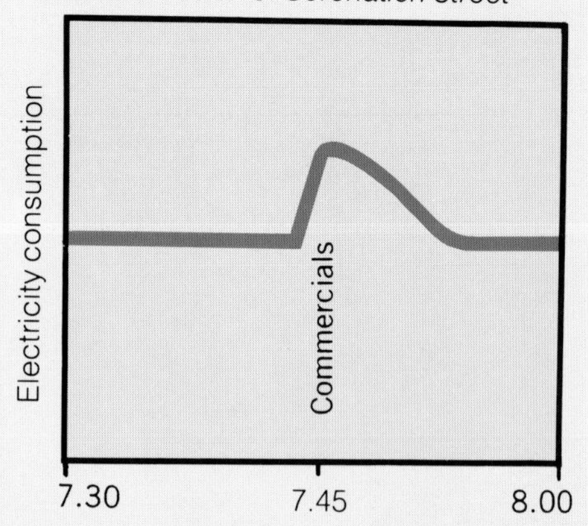

FROM THOUSANDS OF WORDS TO THREE

When a company has something to sell, they usually go to an advertising agency and ask them to do some commercials or posters for the product. They tell the agency everything there is to know about the product. If it's something as complicated as a car there will be thousands and thousands of words explaining what's so good about it. Even if it's something quite simple, like a tin of beans or a packet of crisps, there'll be pages of information about what makes them special and what the company would like to say about their product.

On top of all this, there'll be lots of information gathered by asking hundreds of people what would make them buy a tin of beans or a packet of crisps: whether they'd buy them if the advertising said they were fruitier, or spicier or crunchier or saltier, or whatever.

The advertising agency then cuts these thousands of words down to about 3 or 4 pages. This is called the 'brief'. It tries to summarise what's good about the product and what makes it different from other similar products. It will also say what kinds of people are most likely to buy this kind of product – young people or older people, businessmen/women or whatever – so that the advert will be made with these sorts of people in mind.

Then the brief is handed over to a department within the advertising agency called the 'Creative Department'. The people in the Creative Department have to think up an advert – the words and pictures – using the information in the brief. After all those thousands of words, the Creative Department may think up a snappy slogan which is as short as 'Beanz Meanz Heinz' or 'Milk Delivers Bottle'.

A good slogan can get across all the information, but quickly. It works a bit like a poem. Read a poem and then try explaining what the poem is saying in your own words and you'll find it takes much longer. That's because when the person started to write the poem, they might have been trying to say something quite long and complicated. They then worked out the neatest and most vivid way that they could get it all down on paper.

Poets, like advertisers, sometimes use tricks with words. Here's a verse from a poem that uses language in a similar way to some of the advertising slogans we'll be looking at later.

This poem uses rhyme: crying, sighing, flying. Slogans often use rhyme. For some reason, we all like to hear words that rhyme and it certainly makes things easier for us to remember. The poem also uses words that begin with the same letter or have the same 'sound' in them: "*s*inging, *s*ighing, Trium*ph*antly *fl*ying." This is called alliteration, and slogans often use it. It's difficult to explain how it works, but it seems to make a poem or advertising slogan sound more memorable or funny.

Manufacturer's brief to agency and research material.

Agency brief to Creative Department.

BEANZ
MEANZ
HEINZ

Advertising campaign: commercial, posters, adverts, all linked by three words.

Cackling, crying,
Singing, sighing,
Triumphantly flying,
Magical birds.

Brian Alderson

But how do you make a few words about something as boring as a chocolate biscuit interesting enough for people to remember? Here are a few lines which might have stuck in your mind.

P-P-PICK UP A PENGUIN

This line advertising chocolate biscuits has been around for years and years, probably because it's very effective. A lot of people can still remember the adverts for Penguin they saw twenty years ago, and if you offer them a Penguin biscuit they often say 'P-P-Pick up a Penguin!' because it makes them laugh.

Like all the best advertising slogans, it's really simple. If it just said 'Pick-up-a-Penguin' it wouldn't be half as good. Making it P-P-Pick up a Penguin not only means the line becomes funny but also gets so many P sounds into it that they all seem to lead up to the word 'Penguin.' It's impossible to say the line without emphasising the last word. Try saying it with and without the P-P and you'll hear the difference.

The rules this one breaks are the rules of common-sense. The word 'Pick' only has one P at the start and putting three there is really silly. But it works.

"Tonight's big feature"
"Pick of picnic snacks"
"Give them a real break"
"Just my cup of tea"
"A bite at bedtime"
P.P.Pick up a
PENGUIN
EVEN BETTER VALUE
milk chocolate sandwich biscuits
Cream-filled crispy biscuit—milk chocolate covered—from Macdonalds of Glasgow who bake the best biscuits

Penguin used to use lots of slogans.
Now they use only one

MY MATE MARMITE

'Marmite is a part of your life just like your friends are part of your life.' That's what this line is trying to say.

'MY MATE' and 'MARMITE' sound almost the same. They don't quite rhyme but that doesn't matter. The line is more memorable because the words *don't* quite rhyme. That's a common thing with good advertising lines: they don't do quite what you expect them to do.

Of course, this slogan uses alliteration: four M's in three words!

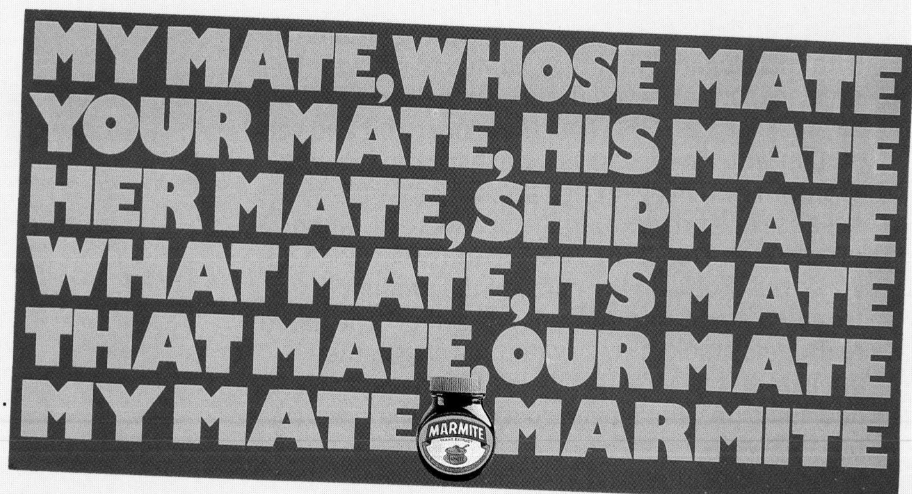

BEANZ MEANZ HEINZ

When Heinz first started using this slogan, their baked beans were already the most popular in the country. What the advertising had to do was make the most of that fact, to make sure they carried on being so popular. So it's quite easy to see how the Creative Department worked from the information that lots of people already ate a lot of Heinz beans, to the idea that 'Beans means Heinz'. That isn't bad: the words nearly rhyme with each other. But they then made the line even better by changing the spelling of Beans and means: Beanz Meanz Heinz. This does two things. First it links the three words much more closely together. The idea is that Beans = Heinz. Look, it says, they're even spelt the same! Secondly, it looks like a spelling mistake that a young child would make and probably get told off for. This adds a bit of cheek and charm to the line. In the original 'Beanz Meanz Heinz' poster, the line was written in chalk on a blackboard. Doing this puts Heinz on the same side as the cheeky kid who's written a badly spelt message on the school blackboard.

DON'T SAY YES, SAY YOP

YOP is a yoghurt drink with a funny name.

It isn't difficult to see how the advertisers came up with this slogan. What they wanted to say was 'Next time anybody asks you if you want a drink don't just say yes, ask for YOP'. Trim that down a bit and you end up with the slogan as it appeared on television. It uses alliteration again. It's also very easy to say because of its rhythm. In the commercial, when people are asked if they want a drink they don't say 'Yes', but 'Yop'. So the name of the product is repeated about *twenty times* altogether! The name really gets stuck in your brain. The slogan then appears on the screen at the end of the commercial, and sums up what's been going on in the simplest possible way.

Like lots of other slogans, 'DON'T SAY YES SAY YOP' doesn't actually tell you anything about the product it's advertising. It doesn't say YOP is tasty and refreshing. All it wants to do is get the name YOP stuck in your mind so that when you see it in the shop, you're tempted to buy it, rather than something you've never heard of. These sorts of slogan are often made up for products like food or drink where there really isn't much difference between one make and another. Advertisers don't even try to persuade you that there is. What they're really trying to do is to get you to remember the name.

I've gone on long enough. My brief was to tell bit about how words 'sell' and then get you to do something. So, now it's your turn . . . '

TOSHIBA ARE PROUD TO SPONSOR THE WALES v FRANCE INTERNATIONAL.

ALL RIGHT TOSH, GOTTA TOSHIBA?

Toshiba make hi-fis and televisions. This is the slogan they've been using on their posters and television commercials. The brief for this advertising line probably went something like this: 'Toshiba make all sorts of very good tellys and hi-fis but the trouble is nobody has ever heard of them. Please come up with something that makes the name Toshiba stick in people's minds. When they go into a shop they must think, "Oh yes, Toshiba, I've heard of them. They make good hi-fis;" instead of: "Toshiba? That's a funny name. Never heard of them."

- How does the slogan make the name Toshiba stick in people's minds? Does it use rhyme/rhythm/ alliteration/repetition?
- What sort of people do you think the advertising line is trying to appeal to? Young people? Old people?

Here are some briefs for advertising ideas for you to have a go at. Bear in mind all the things you can use: rhyme, rhythm, alliteration, jokes, everyday words and phrases.

Shell petrol doesn't make smelly fumes when you use it in your car.

Clue: think if there are any words in this brief that rhyme and see what you can do with them.

There isn't any other rice pudding as good as St. Ivel.

Clue: think of words that mean competitor or someone trying to be as good as you are. Or think of words that rhyme with 'rice'.

There aren't any right or wrong answers to these briefs!

Tips for Success

- You will want to use some or all of these in your slogan: rhyme, rhythm, alliteration, repetition.
- Remember that the slogan must make people remember the *name* of the chocolate bar.
- Remember that your slogan and commercial must appeal to 8–12 year-olds.

CHAMPS

After years of research, a company which makes chocolates has come up with an idea for a new kind of chocolate bar.

You all work as copywriters in the Creative Department of the agency which is designing the advertising campaign. The information you have been given on these chocolate bars is as follows:

— They are very long sticks of milk chocolate with chewy toffee inside.
— They will have a brightly coloured wrapper. Each wrapper will contain 2 sticks.
— They will mainly be bought by children aged 8–12.
— They will almost certainly be called CHAMPS.

On your own

Each of you must think up a clever/funny/memorable advertising slogan for CHAMPS. You must also come up with some possible ideas for a poster and a television commercial. (You can draw the commercial as a series of very rough pictures. Write the 'storyline' underneath. You must include your slogan in the end frame of the commercial.)

In groups

Get into groups of five or so. Spend some time looking carefully at each other's slogans and ideas. Agree on the *best* slogan. Work together on improving the poster or commercial, if necessary.

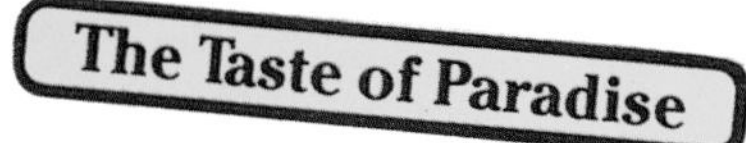
The Taste of Paradise

You now have to prepare a group presentation to the class explaining why you think your group's slogan and commercial or poster should be put forward to the company.

As a class

Listen to all the presentations. The Managing Director of the agency (your teacher) will then decide which should be put forward to the company.

FULL OF
EASTERN PROMISE

PLAY POWER

In this unit you will be reading a short play called *Julian*, written by Ray Jenkins. At certain moments you will be asked how you think the story of the play will develop and how the characters will behave. By working on the script in this way, you will begin to understand what makes a good playscript – and a good playwright.

you will be . . . .

- **Reading aloud**
- **Sharing ideas**
- **Role playing and improvisation**
- **Writing a playscript**

Read the play in groups. There are seven characters.

JULIAN
BY RAY JENKINS

Finch	Julian
Jenny	Sandie
Lee	Alex
Ally	

The play is set in an abandoned church in the centre of a city some distance from a motorway flyover. You can hear the drone of traffic in the distance and then voices outside.

Ally It's dark
Sandie *whispering* Where are we going Finch?
Finch I told you!
Sandie You didn't.
Finch: I told Lee!
Sandie Where are we going Lee?
Lee Sh!
Ally I'm cold!
Lee Keep in and shut up!
Finch *hard* We'll get him in here. We'll get him this time!
Sandie We can't go in there!
Finch I said we can.
Sandie We ain't allowed.
Finch Lee – tell her . . .
Lee *half-hearted* It's all right. Just shut up, Sandie, will you.

The door is pushed open and Finch, Sandie, Lee and Ally look through it.

Finch See! Not locked. What's not locked means you can go in – dunnit? It's open.
Sandie But . . . it's a church!
Finch You'll grow up to be a genius –
Lee If she ain't careful. We going in?
Finch Quiet – right? Dead quiet.

They come into the church.

Lee Ain't it old!
Sandie *whispering* And dusty. Look at them cobwebs.
Finch Uuuuuuuuhhhhhhhh! I'm a spider! *Sandie shrieks* Shut up!
Ally I'm cold.
Lee Put your hands in your pockets then!
Ally I'm still cold . . . I want to go home, Lee.
Finch Why d'you bring her?

Tips for Success

When you read the play . . .

- Concentrate on your part. Listen for your cue.
- Don't speak too fast. Put as much expression into your voice as you can. Sometimes the playwright tells you how to say the line e.g., *hard*, *whispering*.
- Don't rush other people. Let them read at their own pace.
- Try reading the play straight through after you have read it through in sections and talked about it.

USEFUL WORDS

script: the words which are spoken by the actors in a play.

cue: the line or lines which remind an actor or actress when it is their turn to speak next.

Lee I had to. Mum's working today.

Sandie Them statues . . .

Finch All that coloured glass. Somebody ought to put a brick through the lot!

Lee They would of. But it's all covered up with wire outside.

Sandie They're all right. I like them.

Finch They're old!

Lee I'm the queen of the castle . . .

Finch Try falling and breaking your neck then missis!

Lee Three . . . four . . . five statues and me.

Sandie *giggling nervously* Which one's God?

Finch It's unholy.

Lee What d'you mean Finch?

Finch You can say what you like – it's not holy anymore. To make a church holy you got to consecrate . . .

Lee Constipate?

Finch I'm talking. To make it unholy. You know – use it like a warehouse or summat – you got to unconsecrate it.

Lee How?

Finch . . . Dunno.

Sandie A bishop comes and locks the door.

Finch Well he didn't make a very good job of it did he? *Softly* We'll get him in here.

Lee Who – the bishop?

Finch Ju-li-an . . . That kid Julian . . . I hate that name.

Sandie Why Finch?

Finch I just do, tha's why.

Sandie You gotta have a reason.

Finch You talking to me.

Sandie *pausing* No, Finch.

Finch Well just don't, that's all. I don't have to have a reason – right? I do things.

Lee So do I, Finch.

Sandie So do I.

Ally *from off stage* So do I . . . Finch.

Finch That's alright then. Gis the torch, Lee.

He shines the beam upwards.

Look at that little lot!

Lee Phew.

Sandie In'it lovely!

Ally It's only glass windows.

Finch Old genius thinks they're lovely – don't you, genius?

Sandie It's St George and the Dragon. *Reading slowly* To honour those . . . who fell in two world wars. All them names.

Finch It ain't got mine there. Finch.

Sandie Our uncle got his leg bombed off in the war, didn't he Lee?

Lee Not in these wars, stupid. He went to some islands. You was only little.

Finch You don't know nothing.

Sandie I know Uncle Jim's only got one leg.

Finch Then tha's his fault then, in'it?

Lee Where's Ally?

Sandie Ally! Ally!

Lee Ally?

Sandie She's gone!
Finch What d'you have to bring her for?
Lee Ain't my fault is it!
Finch Then why d'you bring her?
Lee If she didn't come I couldn't! I got to look after her.
Finch You're doing a good job then mate!
Lee She's my sister . . .
Finch You know what you are?
Lee She's my sister.
Finch You're a baby sitter.
Lee Ally!
Finch A baby sitter.
Lee Why don't you shut up?
Finch What did you say?
Lee Stop it Finch . . . Get off me . . . Let go!
Sandie Leave him alone.
Lee You're hurting.
Sandie Leave him!
Finch What did you say. Just say it.
Lee *low* Shut up.
Finch Louder.
Lee *low* Shut up.
Finch Can't hear you . . . I'm listening . . . All my ears wide open. No guts have you! Just remember 'Baby Sitter' you ain't big enough, old enough or ugly enough to do anything about it. You're a dead loss – what are you?
Lee Ow. A dead loss.
Finch And next time I'll . . .
Ally *far off* Lee . . .
Sandie There she is.
Ally *high up* Lee . . .
Lee Come down off there! You hear!
Sandie Careful.
Ally I found something . . .
Lee Come down. I'll murder you.
Sandie What you got?
Ally If you don't murder me I'll come down. And I'll show you.
Lee Alright then. Be careful.

Ally climbs down.

Sandie What is it?
Ally If you won't hurt it . . .
Sandie What?
Ally Look.
Finch It's a cat.
Ally It's a kitten. It's a baby.
Finch Look, its eyes are shut.
Sandie Isn't it black?
Lee Where d'you find it?
Ally Up there. It was on a window sill . . . Couldn't get down . . . Poor thing.
Lee If you'd fallen down . . .
Finch Let's have a look.
Ally No. You hurt things.
Finch Just a look little girl . . . Look at his little paws . . . He's opening his eyes.
Lee Where's its mum?
Finch Dunno. Maybe it ain't got one. I knew some kids who tied bangers to cats.
Sandie Don't Finch.
Finch I wouldn't. He won't get hurt. Here y'are. Take him home.
Ally *sniffing* Nobody's going to have it. I'm keeping it. It's mine.
Finch That kid's going to grow up all bats – fly round her bedroom on a broomstick that one will. She oughta have a cat.
Lee She's my sister.

Finch Then you can fly together – can't you?

There's a loud whistle from outside.

Finch *fiercely* Sh!

Silence. Then the whistle is repeated twice.

Finch It's Jenny and Alex. Let them in.

There are running steps outside. Then the door is opened.

Finch Where's Alex?
Jenny *breathless* he's coming. We got him here. He's coming . . .
Lee How d'you do it?
Finch You do what I said?
Jenny Yeh! But I reckon he knows it's a trap.
Finch How?
Jenny But he's still coming. He's on his own as well.

Two more whistles are heard from outside.

Finch Right . . . OK . . . Everybody hide. He see you come in here, Jen?
Jenny No.
Finch Right. Hide. Don't come out till I says. Right. Then you slam the door and you get against it Lee. OK . . . Keep the torch off till I says.
All Right . . . OK.

Silence

Pause here and think back over what you have read.

[1] As a group, discuss these questions:

— Finch is the gang leader. What has happened in the play so far to show you that he is?

— How old do you think these five characters are?

— What have you noticed about the way the script is set out? Does it help you to read it?

— What have you noticed about the way the characters speak? Does it make them seem more real?

— If a film was made of the play, how would it begin? What would the church look like?

— If the play was put on in a theatre, what would the set look like? Where would the door and windows be?

[2] A play builds up excitement and tension by making you wonder what will happen next.

Spend a few moments sharing your ideas about what you think is going to happen once Julian is trapped inside the church. Are there any clues in the script you've read so far? Also, share your ideas about what kind of person you think Julian will be.

[3] Individually, jot down some brief notes about each character. What have you discovered so far about their personalities? Can you picture what they look like? You can add to this list as you read the rest of the play.

Now read on . . .

Finch *whispering* Where's that kid with the cat?
Lee *whispering* Dunno.
Finch *whispering* If she mucks this up I'll . . .
The door opens and Julian enters.
Julian Hey!
Finch Hey!
Julian Where are you?
Finch Behind you! *There's a short scuffle in the dark. The door slams.*
Julian *calmly* Finch?
Finch Ju-li-an.
Julian D'you mind not shining that thing in my eyes.
Finch Three batteries. Rechargeable.
Julian It hurts.
Finch Good.
Julian Why've you locked that door?
Finch I didn't.
Julian Well one of your 'accomplices' did.
Finch Accomplices – big, big words.
Julian Tell him to open it.
Finch Why?
Julian Because I said.
Finch And what will you do if I don't, Lady Muck?
Julian I'll think of something.
Finch Start thinking.
Julian Do you really want to get hurt?
Finch You and whose army?
Julian Just me.
Finch Try it.
There's a sudden movement. A scuffle begins. The light falls to the floor.
Finch Everybody out. *Footsteps and noise.*
Julian *held* Leave go. Get these nutters off my back.
Finch Alex, you're a coconut. Remember that. *breathless* Down . . .
Julian falls to the floor.
Finch Let him go. Get up . . . Julie-Anne.
Julian *rising* You can't even fight without help.
Jenny I could take you on myself.
Finch Shut up!
Julian Manners.
Finch Shut up as well!
Julian Manners, Finchy.
Finch You're on trial, kid.
Julian You're mad.
Finch You stink – so we're equal.
Julian *angry* I'm going.
Finch You can't get out . . . Till we says.
Alex We blocked the door tha's why.
Jenny Try it.
Finch He's thinking – you can hear the little wheels go round! You staying then?
Julian *mock-calm* Why not?
Lee We ain't going to . . .
Julian Hurt me? You couldn't!
Lee It's like – a game.
Julian Good. I like games.
Finch Sit down. I said sit down! Your ears blocked or something?
Julian Thanks . . . Why don't the rest of you make yourselves at home?
Finch Joker!
Julian I mean – all friends together.
Finch Stay on that door, Alex.
Julian And you Jenny. *mocking* I might run away.
Finch You hold the torch, Sandie.
Sandie No!

Finch Lee!
Lee Hold it, San.
Julian Tch-tch!
Finch Why don't you shut up!
Julian Manners again.
Finch Right, Julie-Anne. Court in session.
Lee Silence in court!
Finch Alright, Lee.
Julian He's the judge!
Finch And I'm the executioner – any odds?
Lee OK? *official* Are you afraid of nothing?
Julian I'm afraid of 'something' – bad English!
Finch Answer him.
Julian I'm afraid . . . yes, sometimes.
Lee What of?
Julian Find out.
Finch We will.
Lee Finch ain't afraid of nothing. Are you Finchy?
Finch Shut up.
Julian Manners.
Finch You say that again and you'll be facing the wrong way from your feet!
Julian *rising* Go on then. *hard* Try it on your own. If you got me in for a fight. Let's fight.
Finch . . . Or dare.
Julian Me and you.
Finch OK.
Julian *Gently* Just a game then.
Finch Truth and Dare.
Julian Me and you.
Finch OK.
Julian I'll do what you want – you do what I want.
Finch OK.
Julian See who's the boss.
Ally Sandie!
Sandie Shut up.
Julian Tch-tch. Manners.
Sandie He's a record got stuck.
Ally My kitten. *troubled* He's gone to sleep.
Lee *whispering* Well don't wake him up then.
Ally *whispering* He's all quiet.
Lee *whispering* Then why don't you go home?
Sandie The doors're shut. She's got to stay with us.
Julian Heads you say – tails me.
Finch Heads you – tails me.
Julian OK . . . Tails . . . Alright – what d'you want me to do?
Finch Break them coloured windows.
Sandie No!
Julian *pauses* All of them?
Finch *triumphant* What you waiting for?

1 Pause again here and discuss whether you think Julian will break the windows. Think about these questions:
— Does he seem to be the sort of boy who would carry out this sort of dare?
— Does he seem afraid of Finch?
— Why might he break them, even if unwillingly?

2 Now think about the other characters.
Do you think they'll all want to see the windows broken?
Are any of them likely to stand up against Finch?

Now read on . . .

Lee Look, Finch –
Finch Scared?
Lee Finch –
Finch Julie-Anne? What you waiting for, little girl?
Julian I'm looking for stones.
Finch By your foot. Shine the torch Sandie . . . Lots of bits of brick, see.
Julian What if I don't?
Finch I'm the boss.
Julian And that's what you want?
Finch That's what I want. Scared?
Lee *frightened* Ally, come here. And you Sandie.
Sandie Don't break the windows. Stop him, Lee.
Lee I ain't doing nothing.
Sandie They belongs to the war . . . and the names.
Julian OK. Here we go.

Stones are thrown. Some miss but there is a noise of breaking glass. Julian breathes hard as he throws. Then there is silence and a pause.

Julian Now do you feel good? . . . Eh?
Finch *awed* I didn't think you had the guts. You done it!
Julian *mocking* Well, I got the guts ain't I?
Lee *scared* Somebody must've heard!
Jenny They must've done.
Ally I wanna go home.
Alex Come on, let's get out.
Julian Stay here!
Lee We gotta go. I gotta take them home.
Julian Stay put. I'm telling you . . . And leave that door alone.
Alex I wasn't going, Julian. Honest.
Julian *calm* You walking out?
Finch They might've heard . . .
Julian Who?
Finch Cops! The vicar! I dunno, do I.
Julian Why didn't you think of that before? It's too late now. You've got to do something for me. Remember?
Finch Leave go my arm.
Julian You agreed.
Finch I told you. Leave go.
Julian I did what you said.
Finch I hate people touching me.
Julian You're still staying here.
Finch Outside.
Julian Here.
Finch Why?
Julian Its my turn to say – that's why! You made an agreement – kid? You do what I say.
Finch You're mad!
Julian You stink. So we're quits . . . . . . Ally.
Ally What?
Julian Come here. Sit down the rest of you. All of you!
Sandie The floor's cold.
Julian You won't be long. *mocking* Silence in court. Your name?
Finch Father Christmas.
Julian You're on trial, kid. Name?
Finch Finch.
Julian Christian name?
Finch What do you want to know that for?
Julian Christian name? . . . Christian name?
Finch Timothy.
Jenny *unbelieving and sniggering* Timothy!
Finch I'll fill you lot in.

Julian Sit down – Timofy . . . Right – Timofy.
Finch Shut up.
Julian But it's your name . . . I always call my friends by their first name. Don't I, Alex?
Alex Yes, Julian.
Finch I ain't your friend, girlie.
Julian But you're still called – Timofy.
Finch Get on with it.
Sandie I'm cold.
Julian You aren't afraid of anything, Finch? Timofy?
Finch No.
Julian Nothing?
Finch No.
Julian Anything I ask you to do – you'll do?
Finch I said so, didn't I!
Julian *to Ally, gently* Can I have your kitten?
Ally He's all asleep.
Julian Just for a minute.
Ally Alright.

Julian See this?
Finch Yes.
Julian What is it?
Finch A cat – blind are you?
Julian Kill it.

There is a shocked silence.

Pause again and discuss what you have read and what you think is going to happen.

1. The children are all shocked by what Julian has asked Finch to do. Did it come as a surprise to *you*?
   - If you guessed what was going to happen, how did you do so? When exactly did you know?
   - If you didn't guess what Julian was going to dare Finch to do, look back over the script, and find where Ray Jenkins may have given clues.

2. There is a power struggle going on between Finch and Julian. At the start of the play, Finch was giving the orders. Look back and decide when Julian starts to take over from Finch. How can you tell? Why is he able to do so?

3. From what you know so far about Finch, do you think he will kill the kitten?

4. If Finch does kill the kitten, what do you think the other characters will say and do? If he doesn't kill the kitten, what do you think will happen?

5. From what you know so far about Finch's gang, do you think they will all remain loyal to Finch, whatever happens?

You might want to add to the notes you made earlier about the various characters.

Now read on . . .

Finch Kill it?
Julian Yes, kill it – Timofy.
Finch What? I . . . I can't.
Julian Scared?
Finch No . . . Yeh, it's alive.
Ally It's mine. I want it back. You can't touch it. Give it me.
Julian Take her away, Lee.

Ally is crying.

Lee *scared* Come on Tiny.
Ally I'm not going home. I want my kitten.
Sandie You can't kill it.
Julian Finch can't.
Sandie You're . . . you're mad.
Julian Ti -mo -fy . . . Not afraid of nothing. Nothing? . . . Only a little kitten?
Finch Give it to us then.
Julian Presenting one tiny, furry, baby kitten. Go on.
Sandie Don't Finch!
Finch Ally. Here y'are.
Ally It's mine! I'm going home. *Ally runs out, with the kitten.*
Julian Finch. You're a dead loss – what are you?
Alex He's a dead loss.
Jenny You're finished, Finch. Ti-mo-fy – I mean. I'm going.

Jenny goes.

Julian And who's boss? Eh? . . . Quite right. Me. Open the door, Alex.

Alex opens the door.

. . . I'm going home, Timofy. You coming Lee?
Lee Yeh. I s'pose so.
Julian Alex?
Alex Yeh.
Julian Sandie? Hey, Finchy! Your Dad's name was Julian. Wasn't it?
Finch How d'you know?
Julian I went round your house. Your mum said. I said I was your friend. He must've been a good bloke . . . Night night Timofy,

The door slams behind Julian.

Finch Why ain't you gone?
Sandie Dunno.
Finch Why don't you go then?
Sandie Look at them poor windows. . . . I don't like that Julian.
Finch You mean you like me.
Sandie A bit.
Finch Why?
Sandie You didn't want to kill the kitten . . . That mad kid did.
Finch I was leader. Now he is.
Sandie I don't care.
Finch It was my gang.
Sandie . . . It's cold. You coming?
Finch *low* My Dad was in the army you know. Over in Ireland. You know what he said?
Sandie I bet he said lots of things.
Finch He said, if you ain't tough . . . you ain't no good. He used to punch me all the time. That's why we left.
Sandie I'm cold. You coming or not?
Finch In a mo.
Sandie Finch?
Finch What?
Sandie I don't reckon your Dad's right. G'night.

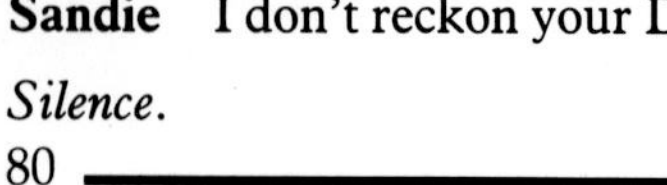

Silence.

Discuss!

1 Talk about how the play ends.
— Were you surprised by how it ended? If so, why? If not, why not?
— Do you think it's a good ending?
— How else could it have ended?
— Why do you think that Ray Jenkins chose to end it in this way?

2 Talk about Finch's character.
— Have your feelings towards Finch changed by the end of the play? In what way?
— Do you think Finch's personality changes during the play? Or is it just that you find out more about him?

3 Talk about Julian's character.
— What are your feelings about him by the end of the play?
— Can you pinpoint moments in the play when your feelings about him begin to change?
— Why do you think he behaves as he does?

4 Compare the notes you've made so far on the other characters. Do you all agree about their personalities, their ages, their looks?

5 Which do you think was the most 'dramatic' moment of the play? When were you most unsure what was going to happen next? When was the biggest turning-point?

Act now!

1 Working as a group, improvise one of these scenes. You know the characters well. Act out what you think they will do and say in the situations.

Jenny/Alex/Julian Improvise the scene in which Jenny and Alex persuade Julian to come to the church.

Jenny/Alex/Julian/Lee What happens as they leave the church? What do they talk about?

Finch/Julian Next day at school Finch and Julian meet. What happens?

Sandie/Lee/Ally Later that evening Sandie comes home. What does she say to Lee?

2 Act out the courtroom scene from where Finch says 'Right, Julie-Anne. Court in Session.' to the end of that section. Concentrate on the tension and excitement in the lines. Add extra lines for some of the characters if you want to.

Write on!

1 You could write up your character notes, perhaps comparing Finch and Julian. Write about what they say and do and what this reveals about them.

2 You could write a short script of your own based on one of the improvisations. You'll need to look at how Ray Jenkins uses language. The words and sentences are often grammatically wrong, because he is trying to capture the way he believes his character would *speak*. But remember, you can only get away with writing down words like 'ain't' and 'dunno' when doing something very special like this.

Tips for Success

When you improvise...

- Think about what the character you are playing would do, not about yourself.
- Listen carefully to the others. Respond to what they say and do.

USEFUL WORDS

improvisation: acting as if you were a certain character and making up the lines they might say.

set: the things which go on the stage and in the background to make a play feel real and let the audience know where the play is taking place.

Picture Books

You may be able to remember the picture books you read or had read to you when you were very young. This unit takes you back to those days. You will be thinking about what makes a good picture book. You will be hearing from a picture book author. You will then have a go at writing your own picture book.

you will be....

- Sharing ideas
- Writing a story
- Presenting information
- Commenting on written texts
- Responding to a writer

Looking back . . .

1 In pairs or groups talk about the picture books you liked when you were young. Did you have a particular favourite? What did you like about it? Do you still have a copy? Did you read it or did your parents read it to you?

The illustrations on the next pages are taken from three different picture books:

For each book decide:

— How old would a child have to be to enjoy the story?
— Would the story read aloud well?
— What do the pictures add to the story? Could they be left out? What part do they play in telling the story?

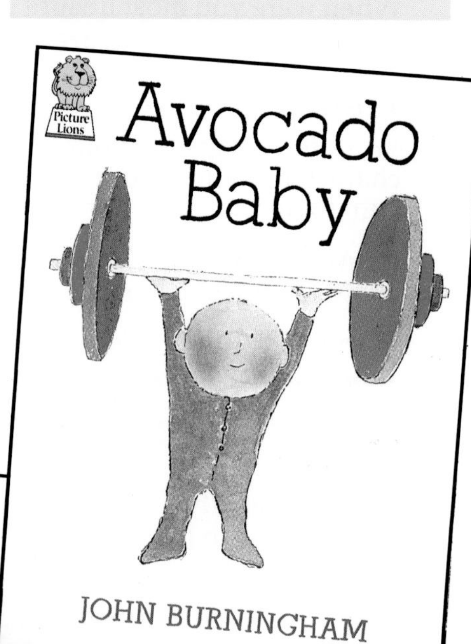

स्पॉट कहां गया?
Eric Hill
A dual-language book

Mog in the dark

Mog thought, what is that?
What is that in the dark?
Is that a mouse?
I can eat a mouse.

It may be a big bad mouse.

a dog.

17

Mog thought, who is that?
Who is that in the dark?
Is that a bird?
Birds are not bad.

10

But it may be a big bird.

It may be a big bird with teeth.
A big bird with teeth can be bad.

11

Avocado Baby

One night a burglar got into the house.

The baby woke up and heard the burglar moving about downstairs.
The baby picked up a broom,

and chased the burglar. The burglar was so frightened at being chased by a baby that he dropped his bag and ran out of the house.

The next day Mr Hargraves put a notice on the gate. "That should keep the burglars away," he said.

BEWARE OF THE BABY

Where's Spot?
स्पॉट कहां गया?

What makes a good picture book?

Now you are going to write a review of a picture book. It will be published in a magazine for parents. You may have a book at home that you could review. If not, borrow one from your local library. You will need to write about:

The story
A brief summary of what happens might be useful.

The illustrations
Do they fit in with the story? Would they appeal to a child?

The age group
Is the story for reading aloud or for children to read themselves? How old would the child-reader need to be?

Value for money
Is the book hardwearing enough for small children to handle? Would a child want to re-read it?

The reviews printed on this page should help you.

Tips for Success

- Read the book carefully before you begin to write.
- Be as brief as possible. Look at how reviewers sum up a book in a few sentences.

Avocado Baby
John Burningham

Cape £5.95
Fontana Picture Lions £1.75

The Hargraves family suffers from poor health. When a new baby is born, Mrs Hargraves has problems feeding it. Then she discovers that the baby likes eating avocado pears. It grows stronger every day and takes on the job of looking after the rest of the family. It frightens off a robber and protects the older children from bully boys.

Children love trying to work out whether the baby is a boy or a girl. John Burningham never lets on in the story or the pictures. Children are also amused by the baby taking on the adult role in the family.

The story is well written and the pictures are colourful, bright and full of detail. A wonderful book to read with infants.

MOG IN THE DARK
Judith Kerr

Illus: by the author
Fontana Picture Lions
48 pp £2.25

Here is a paperback edition of another of the ever popular Judith Kerr 'Mog' adventure books. This one is aimed at beginning readers. The vocabulary is limited to fifty words.

Mog feels very dejected at being left outside in the dark when all that he loves is inside the house. He falls asleep on the branch of a tree and has nightmares about birds with teeth, flying mice, tree-climbing dogs and his ability to fly.

A good book for encouraging children to talk and write about their own dreams, nightmares and fantasies.

Where's Spot?
Eric Hill

Heinemann/Baker Books

Spot surely needs no introduction, appearing as he does in an ever-increasing number of stories and in different languages all over the world. The cheeky dog stars in bright, colourful illustrations to tell a story in language which is simple enough to be followed with pleasure by very young children.

Of all the books, 'Where's Spot?' remains the best. Spot's mum looks for him under a series of flaps and there's a small surprise at the end. The opening flaps are durable enough to stand a constant battering from tiny fingers and the book is available in both hardback and paper covers. Spot is an essential experience of childhood, and one which all children will want to enjoy again and again.

Now meet a picture book writer

Tony Ross writes and illustrates stories for young children. Read what he says about being a picture book writer.

Jayne Potter
Collins Educational
8 Grafton Street
London

Dear Jayne

Thanks for your note. Gosh, it is difficult to write down how I get ideas. Thinking about it, I'm not sure where the ideas come from myself, or what the process is... but I've had a bash.

When I devise a children's picture book, I am lucky enough to do both the writing and the pictures. It is essential that these two elements fit snugly together, as they do with the Pooh stories - written by A A Milne with drawings by E.H.Shepard.
Naturally, the first thing I want, is an idea, a PLOT!
Where do ideas come from?
When a journalist asked this question of John Lennon, he replied; "TESCO'S", which isn't far from the truth. Ideas are all around you. All you need to do is spot them, then bend them to any form you like. Once, I was invited to talk to children at a school, and all the classes were being herded into the hall, where I was waiting. Suddenly a frazzled teacher arrived... "WHERE'S CLASS FOUR?"
Class Four were lost in the corridors somewhere. That was real life, but what a marvellous starting point for a story. Did Class Four enter a hitherto unnoticed room, did the door shut silently, were the walls covered in slime... over to you!
So, look at real life, but look with intent to FIND.
Once real life has handed you the idea, then you must embellish it.
You must form it with a beginning, a middle, and an end. Sometimes you must make up great chunks to make the story flow. Don't be faint hearted. Use your imagination.
IMAGINATION.
Sometimes, I make up stories totally, with NO observation of real life. Once, I asked a group of children to do just that. They said "We don't have any imagination".
So... I said, "Imagine a knock comes at your door - you open it, and there is a cat. 'I've come to dinner.' says he.
What would the cat be wearing?"
At first, the children giggled. Someone said "a black suit". Someone else said "yellow shoes". Then it went mad, and the most marvellous cats were described. MAGIC IMAGINATION! ... From people who thought they had no imagination.

A story I made up like this, without bothering with the constraints of real life, was 'Towser and Sadie's Birthday'.
It is about a cat - Sadie - who asks for the moon as a birthday present. Towser, a crafty dog, fails to get the real moon - it is too far away - but, not wanting to disappoint Sadie, he gives her a white balloon. She knows it's not really the moon, but doesn't say so.
Really, the story is about two people putting the other's feelings first.
In starting this story I had to find something to say, and that was it: two people telling fibs, to save each other's feelings. A simple message, but one not uncommon.
So, LOOK FOR SOMETHING TO SAY.
Then, imagination took over, and my own imagination process was guided by very simple rules that I apply to all my story telling.
They are:

Try to make sure your idea says something worth saying - something that will interest others.

Try to invent interesting characters.

Be 'VERY'. (VERY funny, or VERY frightened, or VERY romantic, or VERY adventurous - whatever you want your story to be, make it 'VERY'. I hope you understand this, because I may be putting it badly, but I think it's VERY important!)

I think a story should start with a big bang, but the most important bit is the ending. I like to end with a surprise. (How often is a promising horror film on TV spoilt by a flat, predictable ending? If you can think of a terrific ending, you've got a terrific story.)

DON'T use too many words. Keep to the point. Don't ever use a word you don't have to. CUT, CUT, CUT!

Use your own natural language. Don't try to imitate 'literature'.

Stick your neck out. Don't be nervous - better to be outrageous than boring. Don't play safe.

Maybe most important of all, ENTERTAIN!

When I sit down to make things up I use the checklist above. (It's not always easy.) As I write for very small children, I must use words and situations that I think they will know, although I do think it is good to toss in the difficulties, because it makes them think, and stretching their minds, stretches their world.
I'm falling into the trap - I'm becoming pompous,I'm becoming boring, I'm using too many words,·my word processordoesn't likeit,,,it towardsssgt465hjmg44$$...
AAAAAAAAAAAAAAAAAGH!

Best wishes,

Tony

Tony Ross

These pages are from *Towser and Sadie's Birthday*, published by Fontana Picture Lions.

TOWSER and Sadie's Birthday

Towser rushed indoors, straight to his playroom. He flung himself into his toybox and flung his toys out. There at the bottom of the toybox was what he was looking for – a big, white balloon.

Sadie was doing a spot of gardening when Towser arrived with his present.
"Happy birthday, Sadie," he said. "Here's your present – just what you wanted."
Sadie examined the balloon. "Is it the *moon*?" she gasped.
Towser nodded. He couldn't quite say, "Yes."
"It's *lovely!*" squealed Sadie.
Towser smiled.

Now it's your turn

You should by now have quite a good idea of the kinds of stories and illustrations that young children like. You have also been given some helpful hints by a children's writer. Now it's up to you to write a picture book of your own.

Before you begin, think about all the points listed below. You could discuss each of them with a partner. Some of them are the kinds of questions a writer like Tony Ross asks himself before he begins to write.

Age group

Is the story going to be read aloud or will the child read it? (If the story is going to be read aloud by a grown-up, you can put *more* words on a page and *harder* words.)

Story

Will the story be funny? Sad? Exciting? Who will the main character be? A child? An animal? A dragon? A witch?

Illustrations

What sort of pictures will you use? Will there be one on each page? (If you find drawing difficult you may decide to have more words and fewer pictures.)

The cover

This is very important. It needs to appeal to parents and children.

Format

If you use A4 paper and fold it in half, this gives an A5 booklet that will be easy to staple together. (You will need to be careful about page order.)

Presentation

Use coloured paper to make your book look more attractive. Some very successful picture books use flaps which the child has to lift up. Others are 'pop-up'.

Type

You will need to make your writing larger than usual, and as neat as possible, so that it can be read by young children. You might want to type out your story.

Begin by writing out the words of your story in full. Then make rough sketches of the illustrations. Redraft your story and redraw your illustrations until you are happy with them. Then prepare the finished book.

She was suprised to hear the frog talk to her. He said, "If you kiss me I will turn into a handsome prince." The princess kissed the frog.

But the frog did not turn into a handsome prince. He became an evil baron. He told the princess he saw her every day and he had fallen in love with her and wanted to marry her.

They went far into another world a world of teddybears

They laughed and played. Rod enjoyed himself so much.

Charlie saw a big shadow.
It was a monster!

"Are you a monster?", said Charlie.
"Yes", said the monster.

Publishing your book

Your book is now printed. But how are you going to tell people about it? To help sell their books, publishers produce catalogues. These contain pictures of each book's cover and a short description of the book.

In groups of five or six, decide on a name for a publishing company. Each member of the group has to then produce a catalogue, containing descriptions of *all* the groups' books, alongside pictures of their covers.

Before you begin, discuss the descriptions you will be writing. How will they differ from the sorts of things you wrote in the reviews? Remember that you are writing for grown-ups and you have to *persuade* them to *buy* the books.

Tips for Success

- A good catalogue entry sells books by being lively and informative.
- Mention anything special about the books. Are they pop-ups? Is the author very famous?

How well did you do?

The best way to find out if your book is a good one, is to show it to young readers. It may be possible for your teacher to arrange a visit to a local primary school.

ORCHARD BOOKS
PICTURE BOOKS

KATIE'S PICTURES
James Mayhew

'*The Haywain* by John Constable. Do not touch,' read Katie. But mischievous Katie couldn't resist touching it, found the painting was real and climbed right into it!

In this amusing and imaginative fantasy a little girl discovers that an art gallery is not quite the dull and stuffy place she expected. Five famous paintings — *The Haywain* by Constable, *Madame Moitessier* by Ingres, Renoir's *Les Parapluies*, Rousseau's *Tropical Storm With a Tiger* and *Dynamic Suprematism* by Malevich — come alive for Katie.

A character children can identify with, lively waterc[...]our illustrations incorporating rep[...] [...]f all the paintings, inf[...] end about each [...] — this book is [...] introduction t[...] children.

£6.25 Oc[...]
215×250m[...]
full colour [...]
1 85213 1[...]

HIPPOS GO OUT
Althea
Pictures by
Bettina Paterson

A follow-up to *Hippos at Home*, here is a week in the life of the hippo family, bustling with everyday activities outside the home. Going to the park, Joe's first day at playschool, a visit to the doctor, a trip to the swimming pool, Saturday morning shopping and many more outings are described through a simple thread of story amplified by speech bubbles.

Althea is well-known to parents and children alike for her sensitive [h]andling of situations all small [...] [wi]ll identify with. And [...] [pict]ures, in [...]

TAKE CARE, LITTLE FISH
Denys Cazet

William is a young bear who sets off to school, dawdles through the woods, drops his school book in the pond, and is surprised to find himself at school with a dead fish in his pocket. Even his teacher — a stork — can't help him with his feelings of dismay. It is up to William to decide what to do with the fish.

How he does so makes a most satisfying ending to a gently humorous, beautifully observed story that will help introduce children to a difficult subject.

ORCHARD BOOKS
PICTURE BOOKS

TED AND ALICE
John Talbot

A holiday! What could be more fun for two retired bears, stuck away in the attic? Ted and Alice pack the camping things, build themselves a car out of old cardboard boxes, and drive away — into a lovely picture of the countryside torn out of a magazine.

John Talbot's teddy bears in their game of makebelieve are exceptionally appealing, and a strong and unusual story is supported by stylish illustrations.

£6.25 September
252×202 mm 32 pages
full colour throughout
[1 8]5213 118 7

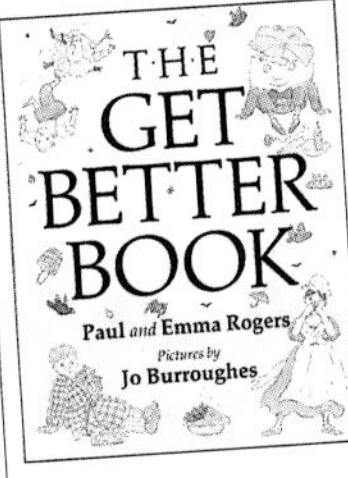

THE GET BETTER BOOK
Paul and Emma Rogers
Pictures by
Jo Burroughes

This appealing book was designed especially for children who are ill in bed, but every small child will love to join Humpty Dumpty and a host of favourite nursery characters as they romp through the warm and imaginative rhyming story.

With the original nursery rhymes set out at the back of the book, this is perfect for reading aloud and sharing.

£6.25 June
252×202 mm 32 pages
full colour throughout
1 85213 049 0

SARAH BULLDOG *and* ROGER FROG
Siobhan Dodds

These two beautifully simple stories follow *Charles Tiger* and *Elizabeth Hen* in Siobhan Dodds' series of animal picture books for the very young.

Fat and cuddly Sarah Bulldog lives in a house full of sounds which every small child will find comfortingly familiar. Sarah is woken up by the 'tweet tweet' of the birds outside her window, and we listen with her to all the morning noises of her family until it is time for breakfast.

Roger Frog is expecting lots of cards and presents from his friends, so he is very sad when nothing arrives for him in the post. Young readers will love to join in the hide-and-seek game Roger's friends play with him, and everyone will enjoy Roger's big birthday surprise.

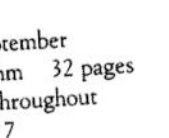

Each £4.95 210×190mm
32 pages full colour throughout
Sarah Bulldog June 1 85213 116 0
Roger Frog October 1 85213 117 9 13

PAT HUTCHINS

Winner of the 1974 Kate Greenaway Medal

Changes, Changes £5.95
A picture book without words based on a versatile set of building blocks.
32pp (1971) *210 × 255 (landscape)* *Fifth impression* *Illustrated in colour* 0 370 01548 7

Clocks and More Clocks £5.95
Mr Higgins has four clocks, which all tell a different time but which are all right. The ingenious reason for this state of affairs will be fully appreciated by children who are learning to tell the time themselves.
32pp (1970) *210 × 255 (landscape)* *Fifth impression* *Illustrated in colour* 0 370 01540 1

Don't Forget the Bacon! £5.50
Words and sounds are delightfully confused in this tale of a small boy and a deceptively simple shopping list.
32pp (1976) *210 × 255 (landscape)* *Fifth impression* *Illustrated in full colour* 0 370 11542 2

The Doorbell Rang £5.25
At first there were plenty of cookies for tea – until the doorbell rang and visitors started arriving…
Shortlisted for the 1986 Emil/Kurt Maschler Award.
32pp (1986) *210 × 255 (landscape)* *Illustrated in full colour* 0 370 30726 7

Good-Night, Owl! £5.95
For details see p. 7
0 370 02016 2

Happy Birthday, Sam £5.50
Sam can't quite reach the light switch or the bathroom taps, but a birthday present from Grandpa solves all his problems.
32pp (1978) *256 × 206* *Fourth impression* *Illustrated in colour* 0 370 30147 1

King Henry's Palace £4.95
Three complete stories in one book, in which the popular King Henry defeats wicked King Boris.
64pp (1983) *235 × 181* *Illustrated in colour* 0 370 30981 2

One-Eyed Jake £5.50
A villainous pirate terrorizes his crew but comes to a bad end when he sinks with his ill-gotten gains.
Commended for the 1979 Kate Greenaway Medal.
32pp (1979) *210 × 255 (landscape)* *Third impression* *Illustrated in full colour* 0 370 30177 3

1 Hunter £5.50
An intriguing counting book in which the reader can spot the hunter's prey long before he does.
32pp (1982) *256 × 206* *Second impression* *Illustrated in full colour* 0 370 30920 0

Rosie's Walk £5.50
For details see p. 7
0 370 00794 8

Picture Books for Children Under 8

The Silver Christmas Tree £5.95
The story of how Squirrel finds the perfect Christmas present for his friends.
32pp (1974) *256 × 206* *Fourth impression* *Illustrated in colour* 0 370 02042 1

The Surprise Party £5.95
Rabbit's important message becomes hilariously changed as it is whispered from one animal to another.
32pp (1970) *210 × 255 (landscape)* *Sixth impression* *Illustrated in colour* 0 370 01521 5

Titch £5.95
For details see p. 7
0 370 01137 6

Tom and Sam £5.95
Jealousy is the cause of trouble between next-door neighbours but their differences are happily resolved.
32pp (1969) *210 × 255 (landscape)* *Fifth impression* *Illustrated in colour* 0 370 01509 6

The Very Worst Monster £5.50
A determined older sister sets out to prove she can be a much worse monster than her new baby brother!
32pp (1985) *210 × 255 (landscape)* *Second impression* *Illustrated in full colour* 0 370 30869 7

* Where's the Baby? £5.50
When Grandma monster comes to visit, the baby is nowhere to be seen, but a trail of sticky foot- and finger-prints soon reveal his whereabouts. Billy, the diabolical hero of *The Very Worst Monster* is back and in outrageously monstrous form!
32pp (1988) *210 × 255 (landscape)* *Illustrated in full colour* 0 370 31177 9

The Wind Blew £5.95
A mischievous wind causes chaos as it snatches up the possessions of the people in the village.
Winner of the 1974 Kate Greenaway Medal.
32pp (1974) *210 × 255 (landscape)* *Fifth impression* *Illustrated in full colour* 0 370 02031 6

You'll Soon Grow into Them, Titch £5.95
For details see p. 7
0 370 30960 X

IRONITE

In this unit you are going to take part in a science fiction adventure. You will be working on your own, in groups and as a whole class to develop the story using writing and talk. You will be making your own logbook entries as the story unfolds.

you will be....

Recounting events

Describing imaginatively

Role-play and improvisation

STAR DATE: 2101
REQUEST No: 261/BZ
RE: MILKY WAY SYSTEM
– PLANET REF. – Z41 P16
PLANET NAME – IRONIT

Its sun only shines on ¾ of the planet.

Cloud structures are multi-coloured because of the effect created by volcanic dust.

PLANET COMPOSITION – IRONITE.
IRON – 50%
GRANITE – 30%
PEAT – 13%
REMAINDER – Coal, Zinc, Sulphur
ATMOSPHERE – as on Earth – oxygen derived from extensive surface vegetation.
⌖ = Suggested Landing Zone

A new drug has been discovered. It is helping people live longer. But all these extra people are using up the Earth's oxygen supply at a terrifying rate. The governments of Earth have united to send out a mission from F.I.S.T. to search for a new planet with continents, seas and fresh air. Twenty spaceships are now heading towards the outer reaches of the galaxy.

One of these spaceships is called Scion. Each of you is one of Scion's crew members. Decide which crew member you are.

THE CREW:

Captain	Geologists
Lieutenant	Technicians
Sub-Lieutenants	Engineers
Computer Programmers	Nurses
Doctor	Scientists
Platoon Commander	Cooks
Botanists	

The journey has already lasted more than a year. You and the rest of the crew have all been in a deep sleep to avoid ageing.
F–L–A–S–H
Suddenly, the spaceship computer, ZIPE (pronounced 'ZIPPY') wakes you up with an urgent message.

Iron ore is the main element of the surface soil. The land is marshy with occasional hills, rivers & forests. There are life forms.

The Dark Quarter.

The two moons are unnamed but they control the movement of the planet.

Write the second entry in your log. Describe your escape. Try to capture the fear and tension so that when, and if, you return to Earth, people who read your log will know what you've been through.

The Captain uses the remaining power from the thrusters to guide the ship towards the surface of the unknown planet. As it crashes, the spaceship ploughs an immense furrow before coming to rest. There is a smell of burning. The ship may explode at any second. Some of the crew are injured and have to be helped out. Flames lick at the shell of the spaceship. The emergency siren wails. OUT! OUT! OUT!

You have each been told to keep a personal logbook. Write your first entry.

- Date it.
- Describe how you feel when you suddenly wake up and hear ZIPE's frightening message.
- Describe your first thoughts about Ironite. What does the information on ZIPE's screen tell you about it?

ZIPE

Mission Time: Year 1/102 days
Standard time: 1500 hrs

URGENT! URGENT!

Rocket guidance thrusters malfunction. Separation from fleet. If present course maintained crashland forecast on Planet Ironite at 1700 hrs.

URGENT! URGENT!

There is no time to lose. The Captain requests information on Ironite from ZIPE.

The ship explodes in a ball of flame but all the crew are safe. They see the surface of Ironite for the first time.

Describe the view in your log. Create a real sense of wonder.

The crew gather together and tend their wounds. They decide that, in order to survive, they are going to need:

FOOD SHELTER CLOTHING WEAPONS

Divide into groups of five or six to discuss the future. How can you begin to meet your needs? What must you do at once? What can you put off? Who should take charge of what? How should duties be shared? How has your role in the crew changed since the crash?

Write a report of the meeting in your log. What decisions were taken? What does the future have in store for you?

LATER . . . As search parties explore Ironite, it becomes clear that there is other life on the planet.

Ice-blue, angular, night creatures, about 15 feet in height. Slow movers. Silent. They come from the direction of the Frozen Sea. They only move north in search of prey and cannot leave their lands for more than forty-eight hours before they melt and die.

You are lost in space. No one knows where you are. The future looks bleak. For what happens next, look out for IRONITE 2!

Write down a number of log entries for these six months. Describe everything important which has happened. Remember that your log entries should be *in role*. If you're the cook, what have you been giving the crew to eat? If you're one of the nurses, what illnesses have you had to treat? If you're a geologist, what rock formations have you discovered?

Six months have passed. Surrounded by strange creatures and many dangers, you have managed to survive. What has happened? Where are you living? How are you using the planet's resources? What are your plans for the future?

Record in your log everything you have discovered about the life forms on Ironite. Draw the creatures as best as you can. Label the drawings if it helps. Describe the creatures' behaviour, and your attempts to communicate with them.

Jet black, slim-bodied, crusty, crawling creatures with fierce red eyes who come from the northern lands. They kill their prey by touch. Their blood is very hot.

Fat, furry, bouncy creatures who seem to populate most of the planet. Some are peaceful and appear to be friendly. They live high in the forest or in holes deep in the earth. They can change into any shape they like.

Tips for Success

- Keep your logbook tidy and organised. Date your entries.
- Use your imagination. If your account ever reaches Earth, it must really show what things were like. It must describe your feelings and the planet in as much detail as possible.
- When you talk to other members of the crew, listen to what they say. Their ideas will help you to develop your own.
- Always act and write *in role*.

Cautionary Rhymes

Poems don't have to use rhyme. But sometimes making lines rhyme can help poets get across what they want to say. In this unit we are going to look at how a special type of poem – the cautionary tale – works. You'll see how it gives a warning, in a light-hearted way, and uses rhyme to bring the message home.

you will be....

- **Solving problems**
- **Writing a poem**

Naughty boys . . .

The poem below is by a famous writer called Hilaire Belloc who wrote a whole book full of *Cautionary Tales*. These were mostly about horrible children who met horrible ends!

Read the poem to yourself or out loud in pairs. It is written in rhyming couplets, which means that each pair of lines rhymes. If you read it in pairs, take it in turns to read two lines each.

Jim

Who ran away from his nurse, and was eaten by a lion

There was a Boy whose name was Jim;
His Friends were very good to him.
They gave him Tea, and Cakes, and Jam,
And slices of delicious Ham,
And Chocolate with pink inside,
And little Tricycles to ride,

And read him Stories through and through,
And even took him to the Zoo –
But there it was the dreadful Fate
Befell him, which I now relate.

You know – at least you *ought* to know,
For I have often told you so –
That Children never are allowed
To leave their Nurses in a Crowd;
Now this was Jim's especial Foible,
He ran away when he was able,
And on this inauspicious day
He slipped his hand and ran away!
He hadn't gone a yard when –
Bang!
With open Jaws, a Lion sprang,
And hungrily began to eat
The Boy: beginning at his feet.

Now just imagine how it feels
When first your toes and then your heels,
And then by gradual degrees,
Your shins and ankles, calves and knees,
Are slowly eaten, bit by bit.

No wonder Jim detested it!
No wonder that he shouted 'Hi!'
The Honest Keeper heard his cry.
Though very fat he almost ran

To help the little gentleman.
'Ponto!' he ordered as he came
(For Ponto was the Lion's name).
'Ponto!' he cried, with angry Frown.
'Let go, Sir! Down, Sir! Put it down!'

The Lion made a sudden Stop,
He let the Dainty Morsel drop,
And slunk reluctant to his Cage,
Snarling with Disappointed Rage

But when he bent him over Jim,
The Honest Keeper's Eyes were dim.
The Lion having reached his Head,
The Miserable Boy was dead!

When Nurse informed his Parents, they
Were more Concerned than I can say:–
His Mother, as She dried her eyes,
Said, 'Well – it gives me no surprise,
He would not do as he was told!'
His Father, who was self-controlled,
Bade all the children round attend
To James' miserable end,
And always keep a-hold of Nurse
For fear of finding something worse.

Hilaire Belloc

. . . *naughty girls*

Here is another poem by Hilaire Belloc about a girl called Matilda. The poem is not in the correct order and some of the words at the end of lines have been left out. Working in pairs, re-arrange the six sections of the poem into the proper order and try to fill in the gaps. Remember that this poem is written, like *Jim,* in rhyming couplets so that each pair of lines rhymes.

Matilda

Who told lies, and was burned to death.

A That night a fire did break out –
You should have heard Matilda –1–!
You should have heard her scream and bawl
And throw the window up and –2–
To people passing in the street –
(The rapidly increasing –3–
Encouraging her to obtain
Their confidence) – but all in vain!
For every time she shouted 'Fire!'
They only answered 'Little –4–!'
And therefore when her Aunt returned,
Matilda, and the house were –5–.

B Matilda told such dreadful lies,
It made one gasp and stretch one's –6–
Her Aunt, who, from her earliest youth,
Had kept a strict regard for truth,
Attempted to believe –7–:
The effort very nearly killed her,

C It happened that a few weeks later
Her Aunt was off to the theatre
To see that interesting play
'The Second Mrs. Tanqueray'.
She had refused to take her –8–
To hear this entertaining piece:
A deprivation just and wise
To punish her for telling –9–.

D And summoned the immediate –10–
Of London's noble fire-brigade.
Within an hour the gallant –11–
Were pouring in on every hand,
From Putney, Hackney Downs and Bow
With courage high and hearts a-glow
They galloped, roaring through the town,
'Matilda's house is burning –12–!'

E And would have done so, had not she
Discovered this infirmity.
For once, towards the close of day,
Matilda, growing tired of –13–,
And finding she was left alone,
Went tiptoe to the telephone.

F Inspired by British cheers and loud
Proceeding from the frenzied –14–,
They ran their ladders through a score
Of windows on the ballroom floor;
And took peculiar pains to souse
The pictures up and down the house,
Until Matilda's Aunt succeeded
In showing them they were not –15–
And even then she had to –16–
To get the men to go away!

Hilaire Belloc

How do these poems work?

Cautionary tales are amusing because they use a mixture of the usual and the unusual, the expected and the unexpected. Many of the rhymes themselves are quite predictable. You probably didn't have too much trouble filling in the blanks in *Matilda*.

The predictable rhymes contrast with surprises in the poems themselves. When reading *Jim,* these things may have surprised you:

— the word 'Bang' on a line by itself
— the lion being called 'Ponto'
— the keeper calling the lion 'Sir'
— Jim being described as a 'dainty morsel'

In the next poem called *The Adventures of Isabel* by Ogden Nash, decide what the surprises are.

The Adventures of Isabel

Isabel met an enormous bear;
Isabel, Isabel, didn't care.
The bear was hungry, the bear was ravenous
The bear's big mouth was cruel and cavernous.
The bear said, Isabel, glad to meet you,
How do, Isabel, now I'll eat you!
Isabel, Isabel didn't worry;
Isabel didn't scream or scurry.
She washed her hands and she straightened her hair up,
Then Isabel quietly ate the bear up.

Once on a night as black as pitch
Isabel met a wicked old witch.
The witch's face was cross and wrinkled,
The witch's gums with teeth were sprinkled.
Ho, ho, Isabel, the old witch crowed,
I'll turn you into an ugly toad!
Isabel, Isabel, didn't worry;
Isabel didn't scream or scurry,
She showed no rage and she showed no rancour,
But she turned the witch into milk and drank her.

Isabel met a hideous giant,
Isabel continued self-reliant.
The giant was hairy, the giant was horrid,
He had one eye in the middle of his forehead.
Good morning, Isabel, the giant said,
I'll grind your bones to make my bread.
Isabel, Isabel, didn't worry;
Isabel didn't scream or scurry.
She nibbled the zwieback that she always fed off,
And when it was gone, she cut the giant's head off.

Isabel met a troublesome doctor
He punched and poked till he really shocked her.
The doctor's talk was of coughs and chills,
And the doctor's satchel bulged with pills.
The doctor said unto Isabel,
Swallow this, it will make you well.
Isabel, Isabel, didn't worry;
Isabel didn't scream or scurry.
She took those pills from the pill-concoctor,
And Isabel calmly cured the doctor.

OGDEN NASH

Of course, cautionary poems don't have to use rhyming couplets. The verses below are from *The Lion and Albert* by Marriott Edgar. Each verse has four lines and the second and the fourth lines rhyme. This seems to make the poem very easy to read aloud.

Here is the part of the poem where the lion has just eaten Albert! Read it with a partner and then decide on the *three* things you like best about it. Note them down and share your ideas with the rest of the class.

Then Pa, who had seen the occurrence,
And didn't know what to do next,
Said 'Mother! Yon lion's 'et Albert',
And Mother said 'Eeh, I am vexed!'

Then Mr and Mrs Ramsbottom –
Quite rightly when all's said and done –
Complained to the Animal Keeper
That the lion had eaten their son.

The Keeper was quite nice about it;
He said 'What a nasty mishap.
Are you sure that it's your boy he's eaten'
Pa said 'Am I sure? There's his cap!'

The Manager had to be sent for
He came and he said 'What's to do?'
Pa said 'Yon lion's 'et Albert,
And him in his Sunday clothes too.'

Then Mother said, 'Right's right, young feller;
I think it's a shame and a sin,
For a lion to go and eat Albert,
And after we've paid to come in.'

The Manager wanted no trouble,
He took out his purse right away,
Saying 'How much to settle the matter?'
And Pa said 'What do you usually pay?'

But mother had turned a bit awkward
When she thought where her Albert had gone.
She said 'No! someone's got to be summonsed' –
So that was decided upon.

Then off they went to the P'lice Station,
In front of the Magistrate chap;
They told 'im what happened to Albert,
And proved it by showing his cap.

The Magistrate gave his opinion
That no one was really to blame
And he said that he hoped the Ramsbottoms
Would have further sons to their name.

At that Mother got proper blazing,
'And thank you, sir, kindly,' said she.
'What waste all our lives raising children
To feed ruddy Lions? Not me!'

Writing your own cautionary poem

You've now looked at four different cautionary poems. You should have a good idea of how and why they work. Now it's your turn to write your own. Use rhyming couplets.

1. Start by deciding who the main character in your poem is going to be. A boy? A girl? Give him or her a name. If you choose a name which it is easy to find words to rhyme with (Mark, Reetha or Jean, for example), you can use the name at the end of a line. If you use one which it's difficult to find rhymes for (Matilda, Sharon or Desmond, for example), you won't be able to do this so easily.

2. Now decide what makes your character particularly naughty or strange.

— Does she never stop talking?
— Does he refuse to talk to anyone?
— Does he pull his sister's hair?
— Does she refuse to brush her teeth?

There are endless possibilities!

3. You're writing a *cautionary* tale. Something terrible has to happen to your character so that your poem acts as a warning to others. Decide what the awful thing is that's going to happen.

4. Write the first rhyming couplet. Don't worry if it isn't completely right – you can come back and change it later.

5. Now write the rest of the poem. Again, don't stop to get each couplet completely right in the first draft. Let your imagination run loose and let the movement of the poem carry you along.

6. Try out your first draft by reading it aloud to yourself and to other people. As you redraft, look for places where an extra couplet will make your meaning clearer or the poem more vivid.

7. Add illustrations to your final version. Produce a class booklet of all the cautionary tales, or a wall display.

Tips for Success

- Remember that you want a mixture of the usual and the unusual in your poem. Plan some surprises. Make sure the people in your poem don't behave too normally!
- Include some real speech or dialogue.
- Don't force the rhymes. Simple rhymes can be very effective.
- Keep reading your poem out loud as you write. You will find new lines and couplets suddenly come to mind.
- Don't be afraid to change the first line of a couplet if you've written it down and can't think of anything to rhyme with it.

Comic characters

In this unit you will be carrying out a survey to discover which comics people read and why. You will be looking closely at some comic characters and giving your own views on them.

you will be....

- Interviewing
- Giving an opinion
- Commenting on written texts

Which comics did you read?

To find out more about the comics you and your friends used to read – and perhaps still read – you need to organise a survey. In a survey, you ask a group of people the same questions and then compare the answers.

- In pairs, think of at least five questions you could ask people of your own age, to find out which comics they read and which comic characters they like best. You may well want to ask which their 'all-time' favourite comic is. You may also want to ask about their favourite comics when they were younger and the stories and characters in them that they liked and disliked.
- Write your questions down and ask an equal number of girls and boys to answer them. If you write your questions and answers as a sort of table, as shown on the opposite page, it makes it easier to record and compare answers. Two columns have been filled in to show you how to do it. You don't need to put in the names of the people you ask but you will want to remember whether they were boys or girls. Try to ask an equal number of boys and girls and remember that the more people you ask, the more useful and accurate your survey will be.

	1 Boy	2 Girl	3	4	5
Which was the first comic you read?	Dandy	Beano			
Which characters did you like in it?	Korky	The Three Bears			
Which comic, if any, do you read most often now?	Roy of the Rovers	Smash Hits			
Which is your favourite character in it?	Hot Shot Hamish	There aren't any			

- When you have finished your survey, look at your results to see what they tell you. Which comics are most popular? Do boys and girls read different comics? Do tastes in comics change as people get older? Are some comics and some characters always popular?
- Finally, write a short report on your findings. You may want to present some of your findings as charts or diagrams. Look at the bar chart below which shows the six most popular comic characters among eleven year old boys. The biggest bar shows the most popular character. Fifteen of the boys questioned said Dennis the Menace was their favourite character.

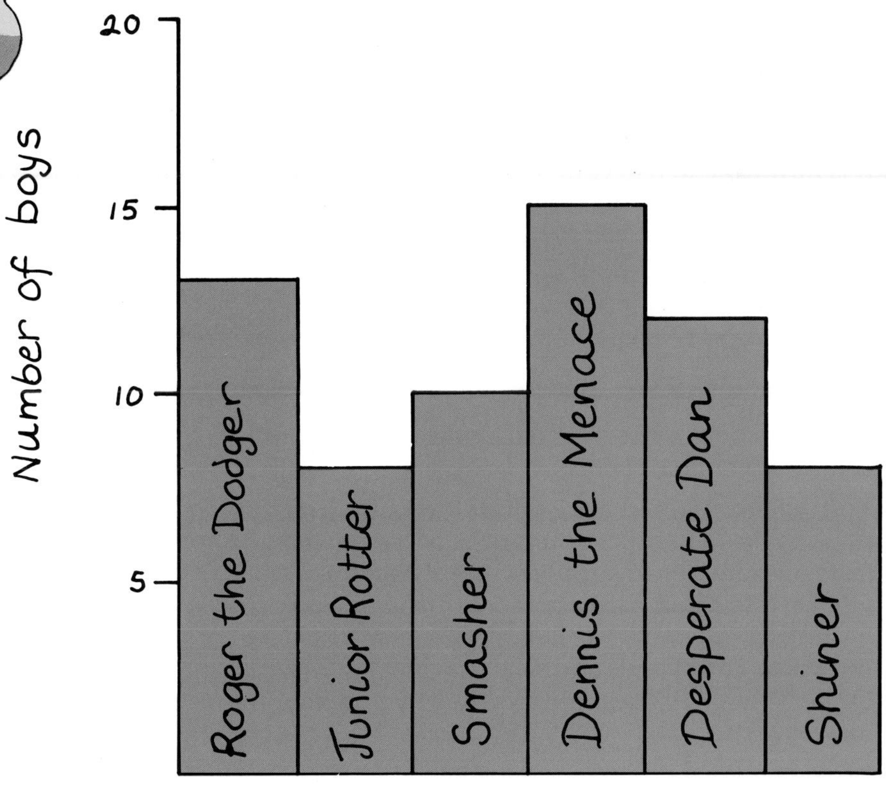

Boys' favourite Comic Characters

Tips for Success

- Keep your questions simple.
- Make a neat record of your answers.
- Be serious, then the people you interview will take your questions seriously.
- Ask each person on their own – not a crowd.

Looking inside

As a class, collect together as many comics as you can. You will know from your survey who reads what, so you can ask people to bring in old copies or 'back-numbers' as they are often called. Younger sisters and brothers may also lend their comics to you.

In groups, look at one comic which you now know is popular with girls and one which you know is popular with boys. For each comic, discuss these questions, making brief notes of your group answers.

1 How many stories have boys in them?

2 How many stories have girls in them?

3 What are the girls like?
weak/strong brave/cowardly clever/stupid ugly/good-looking unkind/kind

4 What are the boys like?
weak/strong brave/cowardly clever/stupid ugly/good-looking unkind/kind

5 What are the stories about?
school life • home life • animals • bullies • tough heroes • weaklings • gangs • crime • fantasy • history • romance • science fiction

6 Do any of the people below come into the stories? If so, how do they behave? What do they look like?
poor people • rich people • old people • fat people • parents • teachers • policemen

7 Do you think that you're like any of the characters in the comics? Which one or ones?

Now, EACH write two or three sentences in answer to the seven questions. Use the notes you made during your discussion as a starting point.

Your survey and report now has some further research to go with it.

Giving your views

It is now time to use your survey, your report and your research to write a short essay which gives your views on comics.

Think what you want to write about. You could write in detail about one comic saying why you think it is good or bad.

or You could give your own views about the way girls or boys are shown in comics.

or You could write in detail about why you think comics are good or bad.

You will need to put across your views as strongly as possible. Wherever you can, you need to include facts or examples to support your arguments. You will need to think hard about your reader. You are writing this piece to be read by someone who does not know your views and who may not agree with them. You have to explain clearly why you hold the views you do.

Whatever you choose to write about:

- Give your writing a title.
- Plan what you are going to say.

There are two kinds of plan you might begin to make. The first is sometimes called a 'bubble plan'. It helps you to think about all the various points you may want to include in your essay. It also helps you add detail to them. A bubble plan is shown at the top of the next page.

The second kind of plan, like the one shown below, is useful when you want to write an essay which compares two things.

Girls in comics	*Boys in comics*
Softies (cry babies)	Tough
Clean	Dirty
Sneaks	Stick together
They don't get into trouble	Always up to mischief
If they're clever, they're ugly	If they're clever, they wear glasses

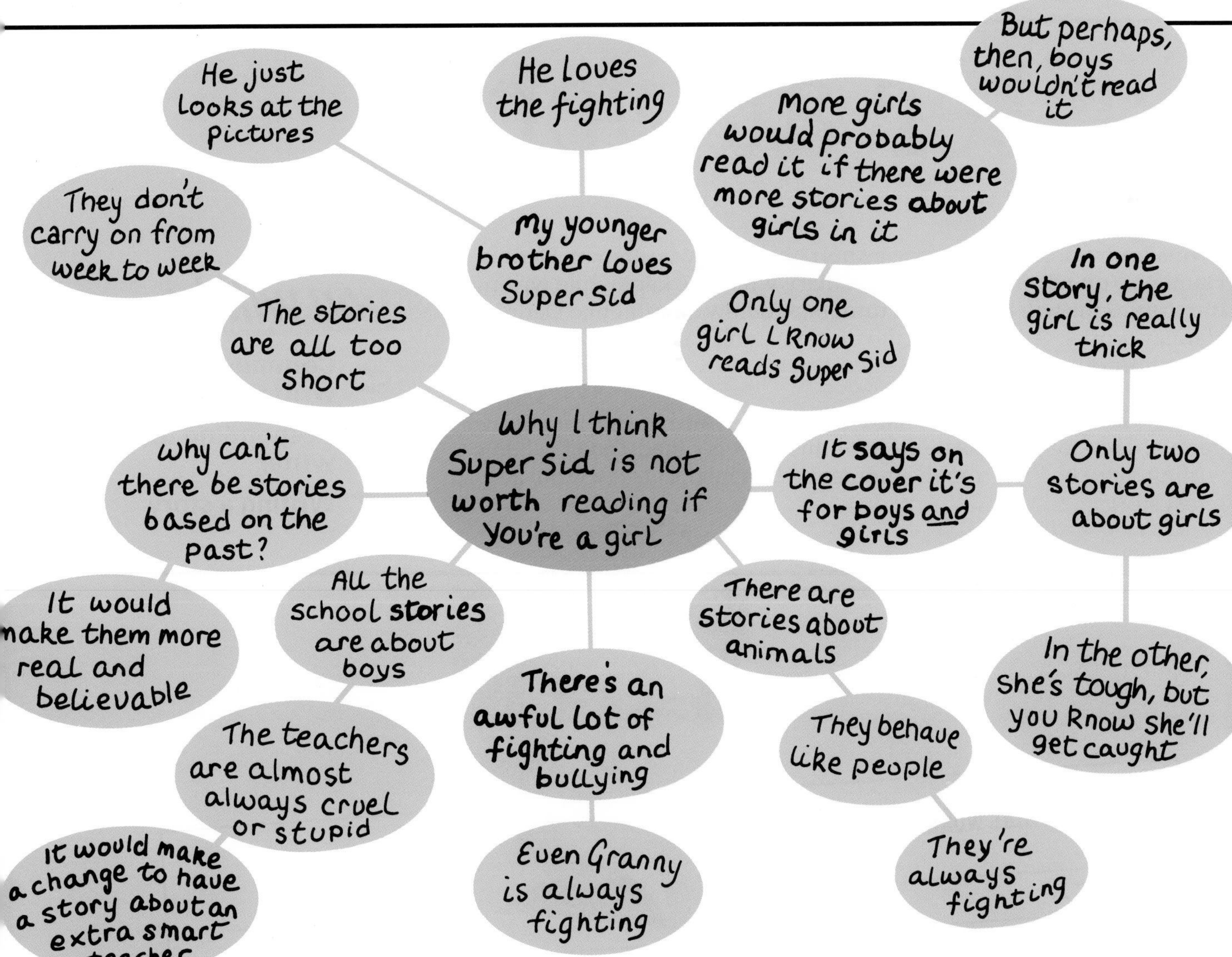

After you've made your plan, you must then decide the order in which you are going to deal with the points you've thought of. It won't be the order in which you first thought of them. You need to organise your arguments so that they make sense to your reader.

Tips for Success

- Think carefully about which subject to choose.
- Plan what you want to say.
- Redraft your writing to make sure you have not missed out anything and that your message is clear.

Writer at work

In this unit you will be reading a short ghost story written by Dennis Hamley. You will also be reading a diary which he kept while writing the story. This will help you to understand how a writer like Dennis Hamley works. At the end of the unit, you will have the chance to write your own ghost story.

Dennis Hamley has written many short stories and novels for young people. The story he has written for this book is called *Time Trial*. His writing diary begins from the moment when he decides to write a ghost story . . .

you will be . . . .

- Commenting on written texts
- Responding to a writer
- Writing a story

TIME TRIAL WORKING DIARY

DAY 1.

I'm going to write a ghost story, even though I don't believe in ghosts. Or, rather, I think I don't.

But I do like ghost stories – reading them and telling them. And there's more to it than just wanting to scare people.

Writers use ghosts a lot and they use them for particular purposes. Often, a ghost will appear in a story so that it can reveal something important about the past to the characters in the story. Once the ghost has revealed the secret about the past, it is released from this world, leaving the characters to sort out the 'unfinished business' which has kept the ghost here. So that's what's going to happen in my story.

Now, what sort of a ghost? A lot of pictures are coming into my mind. Memories of my childhood. For me, that's always the best place to start. The one that today seems clearest is of me riding my bicycle over miles and miles of quiet country roads. My bike was a great friend to me.

Roads can be dangerous places. Perhaps that is why so many stories and legends are set on roads. All those ghostly highwaymen. We never know who is travelling with us . . .

So what about a phantom cyclist? Yes, the more I think about this idea, the more I like it. A phantom cyclist, riding round and round the same road circuit, waiting for the one person to come along who can bring the long bike ride to its end. Yes, I like that a lot.

Now the problems start. What is this endless circuit of road the cyclist is trapped on and why is the cyclist a ghost? The answers to these questions have got to be absolutely right. If they aren't, the story is going to fall flat on its face – though the story can't be true, it *has* to be believable.

Now another memory comes to mind. Because I loved cycling, I read a lot of cycling magazines. I remember long accounts of time trials. Cyclists would gather at the start very early in the morning and set off alone at intervals round a great circle of road up to twenty-five miles in length – a race against the clock. So there is my circle of road – and, I suddenly realise, my title. The word 'time' takes in the idea of ghosts coming out of the past; the word 'trial' suggests somebody is going to have a very nasty time indeed. So it's a title with a double meaning.

This is a very promising start. It isn't often I get a good title before I've even written a word!

But I haven't sorted out why the cyclist is a ghost. Obviously the cyclist was killed while on a time trial but all the ways I can think of at the moment – knocked over by a car, collision with another cyclist, riding at full speed into a wall – just seem silly. For the moment I shall have to leave it that my ghost is a cyclist who met a sad end on a time trial and has been trapped on the course ever since. Well, that's enough to be going on with. The rest will become clear as the story develops.

Enough thinking for one day.

DAY 2

I woke up with something new firmly decided. I now have my central earthly character. He is a boy of twelve, dead keen on bikes, just as I was at his age. Why didn't I think of this yesterday? It's obvious and should have been the first thing I thought of. Still, the obvious sometimes takes a long time to think up.

Anyway, I see my new character living in a town but riding his bike in the country. Which means I have to find a very good excuse to get him out of town and into the country. Another childhood memory helps me here. Now and again I went to stay with my grandmother deep in the country, miles from where I lived. And I remember I went there once because my mother was ill. So there's the excuse for my main character getting away from town.

But that doesn't explain what he has to do with the phantom cyclist. This is a problem. I can picture a scene where my main character meets the phantom cyclist on the road. The ghost recognises him. My hero is the one the ghost has been waiting for. But why? There's a great gap in the story which at the moment I can't seem to fill. And I still haven't written a word!

I have a lot of other things to do today so *Time Trial* will have to take a back seat until tomorrow.

DAY 3

A new day brings a new solution. I have to invent a new character. If the boy is going to his grandparents' house, why shouldn't there be another character already there? I can't see any connection between the grandparents and the cyclist, nor do I like the idea of my main character simply working out some sort of adventure with a person his own age – it wouldn't be right for this sort of story. An uncle – my hero's mother's brother seems about right. He must be quite old by now. Why isn't he married – or at least living away from his parents? Can something have gone wrong with his life? Can this be the connection with the phantom cyclist?

I am still not sure – but I do think I have enough to start writing. Many writers have the whole of their plot worked out before they start writing. I know pupils are often told to do this. It is useful when you begin writing stories. I used to do this too. It took me years to gain the confidence to start stories with only some of the plot worked out. Now I know the rest will become clear as I write.

I need a name for my main character. The name Justin steals into my mind. And so I write my first sentence. 'Justin loved his bike.' I can see his bike in my imagination. It's very like the bike I had as a child – the same make, in fact. Now another memory stirs. I once bought a bike for £3 from a colleague of mine at work. It was very battered but my colleague regarded this heap of old iron with great affection; she called it 'Walter' and insisted that I keep the name. I did – and now, all these years later, it seems very important that Justin's bike has the same name. Perhaps in this story the bicycles are going to be as important characters as the humans – or the ghosts!

DAY 4

Today a picture of my new character is beginning to form. He is tall, dark, mysterious. I call him 'Uncle Henry' because once I had an Uncle Henry who was also tall and dark. After that, all resemblance ends.

Uncle Henry's story begins to emerge. He was once a cyclist, but he gave it up long ago. Why? It must have something to do with the phantom cyclist, but I'm not sure what yet. I do know Uncle Henry is a bit of a fanatic – he does things by extremes. So when he rode a bike it was in competitions and his bike was the very best. When he stops, it is for good. However – and this is important – he mustn't get rid of the bicycle. I want him to store it away carefully so that it can appear later as good as new. I'm sure this is going to be important to the events in the story.

Now I can write some more. I invent the bits about Trevor Stacey and Winston because I want the reader to know just how strongly Justin feels about his bike. The conversation between Justin and his mother about Uncle Henry is important because it starts to move the story forward. But now I've done all the setting up the story can bear. It's time to shift surroundings quickly.

So Justin's delivered to stay with his grandparents in the country. The conversation between Justin's father and the grandparents gives me a chance to reveal something about their life. It also lets me fill in more details about Uncle Henry. When he finally appears I want him to be immediately recognisable.

TIME TRIAL

BY DENNIS HAMLEY

JUSTIN loved his bike. Bought secondhand a year ago, it all added up – with its drop handlebars, racing saddle, alloy frame and ten-speed gears – to the apple of his eye.

'You'll have to call it Walter,' said his elder sister Trish when she saw the make.

'Don't be daft,' said Justin.

But the name stuck.

And with it, Justin's ambitions. To wear the yellow jersey in the Tour de France. To pound round Britain at the head of the field in the Milk Race. No one else shared them. Not long ago, he'd had a fight with Trevor Stacey, who was furious when Justin said that Walter had as much in common with BMX as Grand Prix cars had with prams. While Winston, disappearing up narrow alleyways on rollerskates, would shout, 'You need real personal transport, man.'

'Your uncle used to be crazy about these things,' said his mother. 'Perhaps that's where you get it from.'

'Why doesn't he still like them?' demanded Justin. 'He's not that old.'

'He never said,' replied his mother. 'He just announced one morning he was never going to ride again, greased his bicycle, wrapped it in strips of sacking, slung it from the shed roof and there it's been ever since. More like a shrine than a bike. We thought he might give it to you. That would have saved us a packet.'

Justin was appalled at the waste.

Uncle Henry lived with Justin's grandparents deep in the country. Forty years old now, he had never married. Justin had visited often, he'd seen the bicycle slung there but he'd never thought to ask about it. In any case, Uncle Henry hardly ever spoke.

Now Justin was all attention. Why should his uncle do such a crazy thing?

'He never said,' was his mother's answer. 'But he was very sad about it – never the same afterwards. It wasn't just because he was getting older. He never bought a motor bike; he doesn't drive. He just lives at home with your grandparents, does his work and broods his time away.'

Justin recalled the tall, dark, silent figure. He couldn't remember Uncle Henry ever speaking to him except to grunt greetings and maybe answer a question. A man of mystery. But now, suddenly, a man of mystery worth knowing more about.

* * * *

Justin's chance came sooner than he expected and in a way he would never have wished for. Mum was taken ill suddenly and rushed to hospital. It was late March; school had broken up for Easter, so Justin was packed off to his grandparents while Dad and Trish kept things going at home. Eighty miles into the country Dad drove him, with Walter strapped to the roof rack.

'Miles of country roads to ride on,' said Dad. 'Better than our choked-up, lead-filled sewers.'

Uncle Henry was still at work when they arrived. Granny and Grandad were less than pleased with him and got their irritation off their chests as soon as they saw Dad.

'Can't you have a word with him? He'll have to learn to drive. We've got no bus service any more, the Post Office has gone and even the village shop has closed. We'll be stuck here like prisoners if he doesn't pull himself together.'

'He wouldn't listen to me,' said Dad. 'He only takes notice of his sister. Wait till she's out of hospital.'

Dad left. Justin was shown his familiar room overlooking the vegetable patch with downland stretching beyond. He got himself unpacked, then he went out to look after Walter.

Walter's place was to be in the shed. Grandad unlocked the door and left Justin to stable his charge in the greatest comfort.

When he had done so, he looked up. There was the bicycle, wrapped in sacking and suspended from the ceiling. For the first time Justin looked at it with professional eyes. Yes, even through the shroud, the classic slim lines showed through. Greatly daring, he lifted the sacking and peered underneath. The chainwheel and gears were as new. He looked higher and disturbed the sacking round the frame. Yellow paint and a name. He caught his breath. CLAUD BUTLER. The best. A beautiful handmade machine.

No wonder Uncle Henry could never bring himself to part with it. But why should it hang here, useless? By comparison, Walter looked suddenly dowdy and mass-produced.

Uncle Henry arrived from work at half past six. A van dropped him off at the end of the lane behind the house. He clumped down the back garden in his boots and took them off when he entered the kitchen.

'Hello, Uncle Henry,' said Justin when he came into the living room.

Uncle Henry looked down from his great height.

'You've been in the shed, haven't you?' he said.

Justin shifted uncomfortably.

'Yes,' he muttered.

'Leave it, laddy, leave it,' said Uncle Henry and stalked upstairs to the bathroom. But there was, Justin noticed, no anger in his voice – more a resigned sadness.

★ ★ ★ ★

'And what are you going to do?' said Granny.

'I've brought Walter,' said Justin. 'I'm going to ride everywhere.'

Grandad was very co-operative.

'Here's a map,' he said. 'A bit old but it will do.'

He handed Justin an Ordnance Survey map, dog-eared and strengthened with sellotape where the folds had worn through. It was indeed old – one inch to the mile – and written faintly in ink on the cover was Uncle Henry's name.

'He won't mind,' said Granny.

'Can I get up early tomorrow morning?' asked Justin. 'While it's still quiet, before the traffic starts?'

'My boy, you can come and go exactly as you please,' said Granny.

'Here's a spare key to the shed,' said Grandad.

'A good spin before breakfast works up an appetite,' said Granny. 'We'll look out for you about nine.'

They looked at each other and Justin noticed momentary smiles passing between them. Perhaps they used to talk like this to Henry.

★ ★ ★ ★

In his room, Justin opened out the OS map. He quickly found the village and located the position of the house. Then he looked further afield.

It was obvious that the map had been well used. There were markings all over it. Uncle Henry had certainly got his money's worth. One route in particular was marked in black ink; a cross indicated the start of it three miles away, up on the main road. It stretched east for seven miles to a road junction; turned south to the sea, followed a narrow road along the clifftop for eight miles, then turned inland and finished just half a mile short of the start. It was labelled 'Time Trial Route'.

Justin had heard of time trials. Cycle clubs met early in the morning before the roads were full of traffic, riders set out at intervals and the winner was the one who completed the route in the shortest time. Uncle Henry had obviously loved them. Justin imagined the tall, lean figure crouched over the Claud Butler eating up the miles with a look of dark concentration on his face.

When Justin slept that night, the figure raced through his dreams.

★ ★ ★ ★

Justin rose at six. The morning air struck chill. Low mist covered the fields. He tiptoed downstairs, let himself out through the back door and unlocked the shed.

Before he wheeled Walter out he looked at the Claud Butler. The sacking had been replaced perfectly. Justin had to admit that he'd left it in a bit of a mess. No wonder Uncle Henry knew he'd been there.

Outside, Justin looked up at the house. Uncle Henry stood at an upstairs window. Justin felt the dark eyes boring into the back of his neck as he took Walter up the garden path and into the back lane.

The night before he had resolved that whatever else he did he would use the early mornings to explore the time trial course. That way he would feel the atmosphere. One section per morning – leaving that ominous-looking clifftop section till last. Before he went home, he might time himself over the whole course.

Walter swished easily along as Justin climbed the shallow hill out of the village. After three miles, he stopped. He was at the road junction Uncle Henry had marked as the start. He looked round at the deserted scene – grass verges, where hedges used to be – and peopled them with marshals, timekeepers, waiting riders. He imagined a timekeeper clicking his stopwatch – and suddenly Walter was away, moving silently, swiftly through the mist patches.

DAY 5

The giving of the map to Justin is very important; it's a link between Henry and Justin; it's like a concealed message from Henry to Justin about the past. As I write, I'm very aware that the past and present are becoming mixed up. By deciding to follow the time trial Justin is making a decision to go back into the past. When, next morning, he is at the start of the course I am doing my best to make it seem that the past and the present are existing at the same time in his imagination. This means Justin will be ready to see the ghost.

I have looked forward to this moment for a long time. I look with Justin's eyes across to the figure pedalling alongside him. And when I see who it is, the last major place of the jigsaw falls into piece. It has got to be a woman. Now I know the whole point of the story.

The conversation between Justin and his grandparents will give the reader a clue about where the story is going. It will also have to try and 'cover up' what could seem to be a flaw in the plot. If the central point of the story is what I now know it is going to be – a double secret in Henry's past – how could Henry keep this secret from his own parents whom he is living with? The only thing I can do is be bold and make out that this secretiveness is not strange at all – it is in Henry's character to keep things to himself. So I make Granny say that she knows as much about Henry now as the day he was born and Grandad says how Henry keeps everything bottled up. That's the best I can do. I hope the reader believes in it.

Head down, legs pumping, Justin swept on. This was the life. This was how it ought to be, for ever. He thought of shouting crowds, a yellow jersey on his back, a finishing line beckoning.

And then he realised he was not alone.

He looked to his right. Another rider was beside him, matching him wheel to wheel. Fired by the challenge, Justin stepped up the pace. The rider stayed with him. Impressed, Justin turned back and tried even harder. He stole another glance to his right. She was still there. *She?* He looked again. Yes, there was no doubt. The rider he was racing was a woman.

He shouldn't really be surprised. Women were racing cyclists just as much as men were. And this one really looked the part. Besides, her machine was a Claud Butler.

He slowed. She slowed too. And spoke.

'So you're here at last. It's been a long wait.'

'What do you mean?' said Justin.

'You can't fool me, Henry,' said the woman. She accelerated very fast into a patch of mist ahead. Justin raced after her; for an instant all was grey, cold dampness. Then out again into the light and an empty road stretching in front of him.

Where could she have gone? Obvious. She knew this place like the back of her hand. There must have been a road junction in the mist patch that he'd never noticed.

But what had she said? She'd called him 'Henry'.

Well, so what? If it was Uncle Henry she'd meant, he must have made hundreds of friends in the cycling world over the years. They might be trying to keep in touch even though he'd dropped out. But if she'd mistaken him for Henry, she must be very short-sighted.

He cycled on alone, more slowly now. There was a roaring noise ahead which grew louder. The road sneaked up to a huge roundabout stiff with cars. He dismounted and walked across. Below, traffic pounded along a three-lane motorway. Yes, the OS map was very out-of-date. And the course therefore couldn't still be used for time trials. No rider could get round that lot alive.

That was enough for the first morning. Justin turned round and cycled leisurely back along the way he had come, thinking about the encounter with the woman cyclist.

* * * *

Uncle Henry had already left for work by the time Justin got back. As Justin ate breakfast, he asked his grandparents why Uncle Henry had given up cycling so completely.

'Henry's been my son for forty years,' said Granny. 'And I know as much about him now as I did the day that he was born.'

'He's close,' said Grandad. 'Keeps it all to himself. All bottled up.'

'I know there was an accident once on one of those races he used to go on,' said Granny. 'But it was all cleared up at the inquest. Someone was killed. There was no blame attached to Henry. It was then he hung his bike up in the shed, though. And when I think how hard he worked to pay for it – it's a downright waste and shame.'

That evening, Justin tried hard to talk to Uncle Henry. But his uncle's tongue seemed to be frozen to the roof of his mouth.

* * * *

Justin was up early again the next morning. This time, after looking at the map, he took a short cut to the motorway junction and rejoined the route where he had left it the previous morning.

Now the road left the bare downland. It twisted between trees; branches formed an arched tunnel over Justin's head. Gradually he realised that, once again, Walter's tyres were not the only ones humming along the smooth road.

She was there again, riding beside him. A long, straight descent appeared. As Justin freewheeled, she spoke.

'You're here again, Henry. I knew you would be.'

'I'm not Henry,' said Justin.

'It's all right, Henry. It really is. You must believe that.'

Justin squeezed hard on his brakes. Walter stopped with a scrunch.

'Listen,' he shouted. 'I'm *not* Henry.' Then, as the woman slowed, turned and came back towards him, he added quickly, 'Henry's at home. He never goes on his bike now.'

For the first time, Justin saw the woman properly. Her brown hair was caught up in a racing helmet. She was about twenty. There was an outdoor freshness about her and her grey eyes looked at Justin with open frankness.

'Yes,' she said. 'I can see now that you're not Henry. But this concerns you too. You must bring Henry with you. It's important.'

'Fat chance,' said Justin.

'You must,' said the woman. Then she shot away round the bend at the foot of the hill. Justin followed, expecting to see her in front of him.

But she wasn't there.

'She can't half shift,' he said to himself.

* * * *

That evening Henry clumped in, ate his supper and then sprawled in front of the television. Justin felt he had to speak. It would be hard. Henry's gaze never left the screen. Justin forced himself.

'I met someone who knows you today, Uncle Henry,' he said.

No answer.

'It's a lady. She's a proper cyclist. She's got a super Claud Butler like yours. She says you must believe it's all right. And she wants to see you.'

Uncle Henry said nothing for a moment. Then he turned the sound down, stood, seized both Justin's wrists and fixed him with an angry, dark-eyed stare.

'Don't mock me, laddy,' he hissed. 'Whatever else you do, don't mock me.'

He turned the sound up again and sat back in his chair. But Justin could see that there was anguish in his eyes.

* * * *

At six the next morning, when Justin came out to unlock the shed, he found the door was already open.

Cautiously he looked in – and gasped with surprise. Uncle Henry, his back to him, was carefully unwinding the sacking strips from the Claud Butler which he had taken down from the ceiling. Soon the machine was laid bare in all its mechanical beauty. Uncle Henry, unaware of Justin's presence, spoke out loud.

'I swore I'd never turn a pedal of yours again and I mean it still. Rather than have you accusing me over the years, I'll take a sledgehammer to you.'

Then he put one hand on the handlebars, the other on the saddle. Justin thought he was going to wheel the bicycle outside. But no. Instead, he turned and strode unseeing out of the shed. Justin saw his eyes were bright with tears.

* * * *

This morning was colder and darker. Justin had a lot to think about. His legs felt heavy. Immediately after the time trial finish there was a stiff climb. When he reached the summit, a sharp wind cut into him however hard he pumped his legs along. He would definitely be alone this morning. For miles behind and miles ahead there was no turning, no tree, no cover. There was nowhere she could appear from; nowhere she could disappear into.

Yet suddenly she was there again, riding steadily by his side. It was now not only the wind which chilled him.

'Where have you come from?' he shouted and screeched to an angry halt.

'Where is he?' the girl demanded.

DAY 6

Everything comes in threes. It takes three meetings with the ghost for Justin to understand what it is all about; it takes three attempts for Justin to communicate with Uncle Henry. When Henry's tongue is finally unloosed and he pours out his memories of that dreadful morning years ago, I feel something of the same relief that Henry feels. All this long section turns out to be surprisingly easy. I know what has to be said and I can keep writing without a break.

But there is still a challenge ahead. There has to be a final encounter on the clifftop. This has been at the back of my mind all along. This meeting between Henry, Emmy and Justin will work itself out in ways which I still can't fully grasp. I do know it's going to be difficult to write.

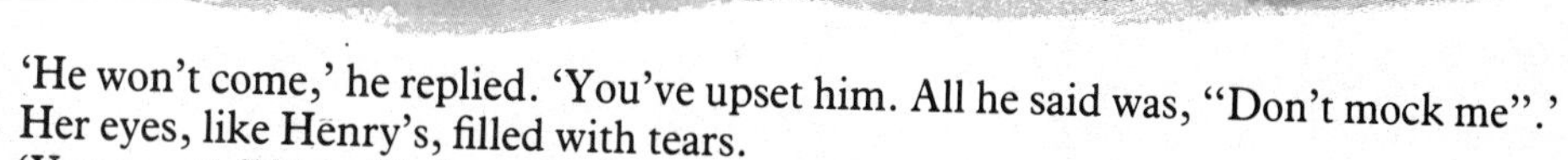

'He won't come,' he replied. 'You've upset him. All he said was, "Don't mock me".'

Her eyes, like Henry's, filled with tears.

'You *must* tell him. He *has* to be here. It's all right. Can't he see that? I don't blame him. Nobody does. He was good to me. I loved him.'

'Who are you?' said Justin. There was a cold feeling in his stomach very close to terror.

'Tell him Emmy wants him. Tell him if he doesn't come tomorrow what happened once will happen again and neither of us will be able to stop it.'

Emmy looked him straight, unnervingly, in the eyes.

'Tell him it concerns you.'

She remounted her bicycle and set off. She dwindled into the distance and suddenly was gone.

He blinked and the cold in his stomach churned round again. It wasn't *who* Emmy was that worried him – but *what*.

* * * *

The day dragged. Justin, badly shaken, rode slowly round the village until he judged it was time for Uncle Henry to be home. Entering the back garden, he saw him at once, polishing the Claud Butler so it gleamed as it must have done in the shop a quarter of a century before. For the first time since Justin had known him, he spoke first.

'Well, what have you got to tell me this time?'

'I met Emmy. She wants you to come tomorrow. If not, what happened before will happen again. And it concerns me. That's what she says.'

Uncle Henry's face was chalk-white and haggard.

'Where do you go each morning?' he said.

'I'm following the time trial course you marked on the map. I divided it into four sections. I've only got the bit by the sea to do.'

'And each time you see her?'

'Yes.'

'*But she's dead*,' groaned Uncle Henry. 'She's been dead these twenty years. Went over the cliff. I could have stopped her.'

Justin's head swam. Suddenly Uncle Henry's tongue seemed to have unloosed. Words gushed out as if dammed up for years.

'We were in the Old Wheelers club. Once a month we time trialled, first thing on Sunday mornings. But that bit over the cliffs was a real killer. A strong wind and you really had to look out for yourself. There was a fence and warning notices but . . . Anyway, on this morning there was a really strong wind and because it was so early it was still blowing off the land. We shouldn't have risked it. But you know what people are like. And it was *our* course, and riders from other clubs were there and we didn't want to look silly in front of them.

'And Emmy? Well, she was . . . I reckon if it hadn't been for this, by now we'd have been – Oh, what's the use of wondering? Anyway, the women riders set off first so we wouldn't catch them too easily and then it was my turn. I felt great – making really good time. But when I reached the clifftop the wind was so strong it nearly had me over. But I kept going. Then I saw Emmy in front of me. Someone to overtake, I thought. The road's never more than ten yards from the edge and here it dipped so you could get up some real speed. She knew I was there – she went like the clappers. Her front wheel must have hit a stone. She tried to brake. The cable snapped – that's what they said at the inquest. She didn't have a hope in hell. She went off the road, over the grass, through the fence and . . .'

Uncle Henry looked at Justin.

'That's why I don't ride any more,' he said.

'But it wasn't your fault,' said Justin. 'She says it wasn't.'

'I thought you'd come back and say that,' said Uncle Henry. 'That's why I've got the bike ready. I'll ride with you tomorrow. On the clifftop section.'

* * * *

That night, Justin couldn't sleep. Images wound round and round inside his head. The ghostly rider trapped on the time trial course, the ominous cliff, the sullen roar of the sea far underneath.

A noise in the middle of the night made him get up and look out of the window. A dark figure stood in the garden, looking up at the sky.

Uncle Henry couldn't sleep either.

* * * *

On this cold, blowy morning, Justin had company. Uncle Henry rode as if he had never been out of the saddle. After ten miles they reached the point where the lane veered off westward towards the clifftop. Now the climb was very stiff indeed. Uncle Henry managed it with hardly a variation in pace; Justin struggled behind.

When he reached the top, the wind hit him like a punch in the face. Suddenly scared, Justin concentrated on looking ahead. Knowing that the sea growled a hundred feet below made his head swim. The wind's force tugged Walter across the road. Justin felt desperate. He wanted to get off, but far ahead he could see Uncle Henry pounding on. The wind roared in his ears.

And then, over the racket, he heard a voice.

'Keep going. You're doing fine.'

It was Emmy. Panic-stricken now that he knew her for what she was, he shrieked.

'Get away from me.'

She stretched out an arm and touched him chillingly on the face. He flinched.

'Don't be afraid. I mean good, not ill.'

Uncle Henry stopped, turned and looked back. His eyes widened. Emmy drifted silently towards him. She took his arm. Uncle Henry also flinched – then recovered and looked her full in the face. For a moment the wind died. Justin heard what they said.

'It wasn't your fault. You could do nothing.'

'I chased you. I sent you out of control. I could have jumped off and grabbed you.'

'Then you would have gone with me.'

'Better if I had.'

'No, Henry,' said Emmy. 'I'm gone. You must look to yourself.'

Uncle Henry hung his head, defeated.

'I have,' he said. 'Look what good it's done me. I could have saved you. There's nothing can alter that.'

He turned away and spoke to Justin.

'Come on, laddy,' he said. 'Time to go.'

'But Uncle Henry . . .' Justin blurted.

'Leave it.' Uncle Henry's voice was harsh. 'I want no ghosts out of the grave to tell me what's what.'

He set off again on the Claud Butler. Justin followed him, pedalling hard.

'She came to see you,' he yelled across the wind. 'She means what she says.'

Uncle Henry rode grimly on. Justin swerved outside him and leant across.

'If ghosts can't get away from this world it means they've got something to finish. Because of you she can't get away.'

No answer.

'Uncle Henry . . .' he shouted despairingly and felt the wind's shock hurl Walter sideways. The lane dipped and turned, following the line of the cliff. Walter lurched onto the grass, slippery with dew.

'Uncle Henry,' Justin shouted again, this time in panic.

He squeezed hard on both brakes. Nothing happened. The cliff edge loomed up. Justin saw only grey, flecked sea far below and felt Walter's frame and pedals buffet and gash his legs as he lost balance and fell.

DAY 7

The thing that worries me as much as anything is Justin's role in all this. I want him to be more than just a messenger boy. He must do more than simply bring Emmy and Henry together. I have made Emmy say 'Tell him it concerns you', without knowing exactly why.

There must be some purpose behind the remark. The reader will be expecting it. I set my two characters riding up the hill in a stiff wind. I am nearly as doubtful about what's going to happen as they are. I'm sure the wind is important, though. It was a big factor in the tragedy in the first place.

Suddenly, the answer comes. What happens on the clifftop is not just going to be an encounter; it is going to be a repetition of the last time. I am going to have to put Justin in real danger.

It all comes back to Uncle Henry's character. He's a stubborn, bitter man. Emmy's words alone would not be enough to make him change. Something else must happen if he is to accept that he is not to blame for her death. There has to be a rescue which this time is successful. Rescuing Justin and risking his own life will make up for the guilt Henry feels about the past. Now he can accept Emmy's forgiveness and Emmy can leave this world for ever. She is free. She has given Henry another chance to prove himself. He has taken it and she can go.

Good. But I can't just leave Justin and Henry there.

I have to round the story off nicely. To do this I'll use things which have already been mentioned. I remember the earlier complaints of Granny and Grandad. By making Henry say he's going to learn to drive I can let it be known that from now on he's going to live a proper life. The best way of starting this new life is to get rid of the Claud Butler; he has no need of such memories any more. Giving the bike to Justin makes up for the loss of Walter. It also makes me feel better about how I treated my hero!

So that's it. First draft finished.

'Uncle He . . .' he started in a last, hopeless wail, as he slithered over the edge.

And then a grip of extraordinary strength seized his ankle. Perilously long afterwards, another pull came at his waist – then a moment's unbearable tension between Uncle Henry's strength and the force dragging him down.

'Let go of the bike,' Uncle Henry jerked out through gritted teeth.

Numbly, Justin did so. A pedal grazed his leg in mute farewell as Walter slowly slid over and crashed downwards, hitting the cliff side several times on its journey.

Now Uncle Henry could use all his strength to save Justin. They pulled themselves up, Uncle Henry sweating, Justin ice-cold but with tears starting behind his eyes.

'Walter . . .' was all he could say.

And suddenly Emmy was with them.

'You've made amends,' she said. 'By rescuing him, you've rescued me.'

Uncle Henry stared at her, as if fixing the sight in his mind for ever.

'Goodbye, Emmy,' he said at last. 'You can rest now.'

'I told the boy it concerned him,' said Emmy and before their eyes she melted away.

There was a profound silence for some minutes as the two stood together at the windy cliff edge, each thinking his own thoughts. Then Uncle Henry spoke.

'Time to get you home,' he said. 'We'll walk to the nearest house and phone for a taxi.'

Justin began to feel the pain from his cuts and bruises and the still greater pain of Walter's loss. Uncle Henry seemed to know what was on his mind.

'Bikes come and go,' he said. 'People don't. I shall never ride again. Take this. It's yours.'

And he pushed the Claud Butler into Justin's hands.

For a moment Justin was speechless.

'But what will *you* do?' he managed at last.

'Me?' said Uncle Henry. 'It's about time I sorted myself out. Learn to drive, that's what I'm going to do.'

And they trudged companionably together on the first stage of their journey home.

DAY 8

A new day and I look with horror at the twenty sheets of A4 paper covered with crossed out scribble which are the fruits of my labours so far. I have a nasty feeling the real work is just beginning. I do a full word count – 6000. Far too many. It's supposed to be 4000. So I'll have to go through it, cutting out things which aren't essential and hopefully sharpening the story up at the same time.

First I get rid of all the descriptive words which aren't absolutely necessary. This is a short story; descriptions must be kept to a minimum. Everything has to pass a simple test; will the story work without it? If it will, then out it goes. There are casualties I regret. Some pleasing things about Trevor and Winston bite the dust on the first page; Trish says something really rather humorous on the next page. It's not essential and I cross it out. Towards the end of the story, I reluctantly cut a description of the sea as seen from above. It almost made me dizzy as I wrote it.

DAY 9

Now to the word processor. I wrote the first draft by hand, rather than on the word processor, because I still find it very difficult to write straight on to a keyboard. With the whole story there in front of me, it is much easier to edit it and rearrange it on the word processor, though. Everything seems to be going well.

DAY 10

Disaster! While trying a fancy bit of editing I manage to crash the program and lose half my text. Just as well I have a handwritten copy. I must remember to save my text every hundred words or so.

DAY 11

All finished. The story is printed. I read it carefully. 60% pleased. But there is something not quite right about it and I can't place what it is. Individual parts please me but it doesn't quite hang together. What is the problem?

THREE WEEKS LATER
Today I have been in a secondary school working with a first year group. We have read *Time Trial* together. They seemed to like it. We discussed the story for a while. The group promised to think further about it and perhaps write to me.

ANOTHER WEEK LATER
The letters arrive. They all say the same thing, though in different ways. Their basic point is this: the story was half way through before they knew it was a ghost story. Of course. That's exactly what's wrong with it. I knew it was a ghost story from the start; I forgot that no one else would. So back to the desk to find the solution.

The answer, when it comes, is simple. There's no need to alter anything. But I must add. A short prologue would be best – a short paragraph at the start which makes it clear to the reader that a ghost is going to be seen before too long. This will, I hope, add some tension. It should also please the reader because he or she will have some knowledge which the characters in the story haven't got. That's always a good feeling.

Yes, that seems to work. There's a lot more I could do to the story but enough is enough. Someone once said – 'A piece of writing is never finished – it's just that at some time or other you decide to abandon it.' Well, *Time Trial* I'm leaving you to your fate, you're on your own.

TIME TRIAL

BY DENNIS HAMLEY

THE road winds over the downs and through the woods. It skirts perilously close to the cliff. In the early morning you can stand by this road at any point you like and see no one. A stiff breeze stirring the short grass may chill your face. The sound of the growling sea may worry your ears. Sunlight sparkling through the leaves of overhanging trees may startle your eyes. But you will see no one.

Wherever you stand, though, you may hear noises you do not understand. Over the mutter of the sea may come the whirr of fast-turning tyres. Under the moan of the wind there may be the squeak of brakes and the scrunch of wheels. In the dance of shade and sunlight may be a shadow you cannot quite make out.

For there is a cyclist following you. Someone you cannot see rides a bicycle you will never touch – never sleeping, never pausing but waiting, waiting. Yes, the road is haunted. One day the time will come for the cyclist to be seen again. But someone special has to come along the road for that to happen.

★ ★ ★ ★

JUSTIN loved his bike. Bought secondhand a year ago, it all added up – with its drop handlebars, racing saddle, alloy frame and ten-speed gears – to the apple of his eye.

'You'll have to call it Walter,' said his elder sister Trish when she saw the make.

'Don't be daft,' said Justin.

But the name stuck.

And with it, Justin's ambitions. To wear the yellow jersey in the Tour de France. To pound round Britain at the head of the field in the Milk Race. No one else shared them.

When Justin goes to stay with his grandparents he is excited at the chance to ride his new bike around the country lanes. But there's more excitement – and fear – than Justin expects, when a ghostly cyclist reveals the truth about a disastrous bike ride long ago.

TIME TRIAL

BY DENNIS HAMLEY

Thinking about TIME TRIAL

The diamond game you are about to play will help you to decide what you liked best about *Time Trial*.

1. Work in pairs or in groups of three.

2. Look at the nine statements. [*These are printed on page 126 of this book, and are also in the Teacher's Resources.*] Each statement could finish a sentence beginning, 'The best thing about *Time Trial* is . . .'

3. Now agree where to place each statement on the diamond grid below. Have the story open in front of you so that you can refer to it wherever you like.

....

....

....

....

....

The statement which describes what you like **most** about the story should go here.

The statements which you do not have such strong feelings about should go on the three middle lines of the diamond.

The statement which describes what you like **least** about the story should go here.

4. When all pairs and groups have agreed on their diamonds, one person from each pair or group moves on to the next. He or she asks this new group why they placed the statements as they did and they have to justify their decisions.

Write your own ghost story

Try writing your own ghost story now. Think about the tips given to you by Dennis Hamley in his diary.

— Use your ghost to reveal something about the past.

— Work out the main stages in the plot and something about your main characters *before* you start writing.

— Use your memory as well as your imagination. Include people and things in your story which you can remember from your past.

— Write your story over two or three days. This will give you a chance to have fresh ideas as you go along.

— Keep a diary of each day's writing. Put down any problems you come up against and how you solve them. Try to explain how your story is developing.

— Pay great attention to the beginning and end of your story.

— Make sure that your story – even if it couldn't be true – is believable.

It's not fair!

In this unit you will be reading about why many people in the world are hungry. You will then use some of the information to prepare a short talk which gives your own views on the problem.

you will be . . . .

- Presenting information
- Locating and selecting information

Where has all the food gone?

First, read about it . . .

There are a number of charities in Britain which produce leaflets, books, posters and advertisements to tell people like us, who have enough to eat, about the problems of people who are hungry or starving.

Read through the information on the next four pages which is taken from an Oxfam leaflet and a Save the Children book.

Then, prepare a short talk . . .

You are to give a short talk (no more than five minutes) to another class. Your task is to persuade them that there is no need for people in the world today to go hungry. You will need to plan your talk carefully.

1. Decide which facts to include. What information do you want to use from the leaflet and the book? For example, do you want your audience to know that 'eighteen children die of hunger somewhere in the world every minute of every day of every year'? Make notes on the information you are going to include.

2. Think about your audience. How are you going to persuade them that what you say is right? You will need to *organise your arguments carefully* so that they understand the points you are making. You will also need to *support what you say with facts* taken from the pages you've read. Otherwise, your audience will think they are just listening to your own opinions.

3. Practise your talk. You could practise it on a partner. The best idea would be to speak into a tape recorder. Then when you play back your talk, you can decide how to improve it. Remember to look at your notes if you get stuck. Remember to time how long your talk is.

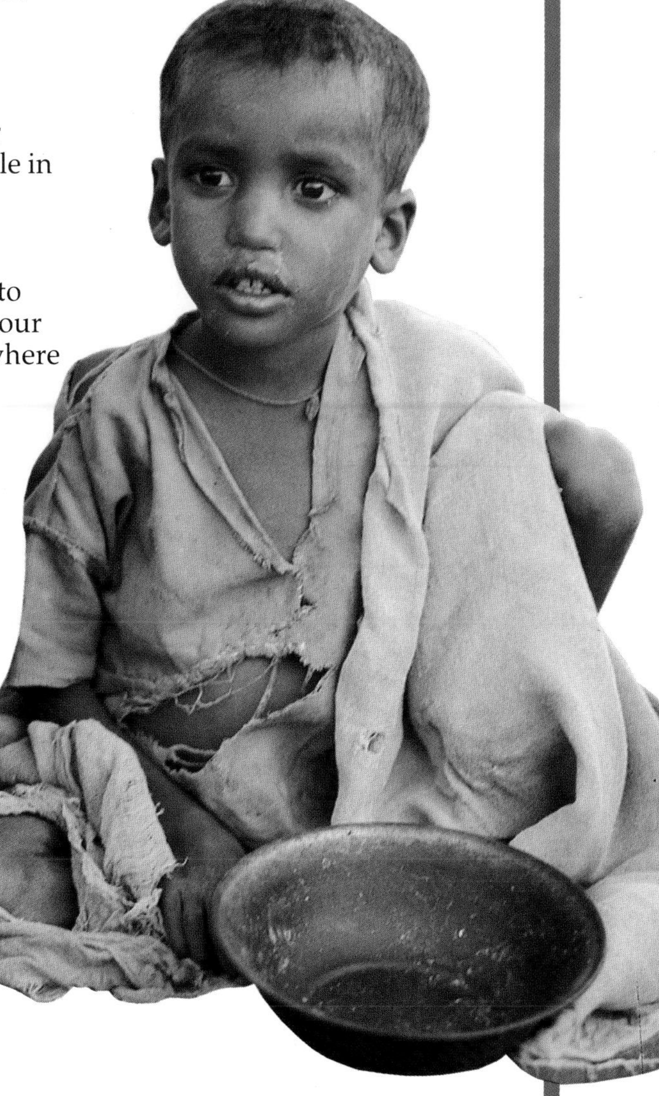

The information on these pages is taken from a leaflet produced by Oxfam. Work in pairs. Read each page through once. Then go through each page again, slowly and carefully, making sure you understood the points being made. (Refer back to page 44 if necessary for help on Skim and Scan reading.) Make sure you can answer the questions.

1. What do 'diet' and 'malnutrition' mean? What are the differences between 'exports' and 'imports'? (Look these words up in a dictionary if necessary.)
2. What are 'cash crops'? Why are they different from 'grain crops'? Write down some examples of grain crops and cash crops. (Hint: look at the map.)
3. Why did Africa start growing cash crops instead of grain crops?
4. Why is grain now imported into Africa?
5. Why can't Africans 'look forward to the day when they will be well-fed'?

2 Is the world short o food, or isn't it

Well, famines certainly happen; the starving children certainly exist. And all too many people whom we never read about in our newspapers go hungry for at least three or four months a year.

Yet the world is not actually short of food. Enough is produced to give everyone a healthy diet. What's more, most countries have the resources - enough land, water, etc. - to feed their people, if they want to.

Why then, do so many people go hungry?

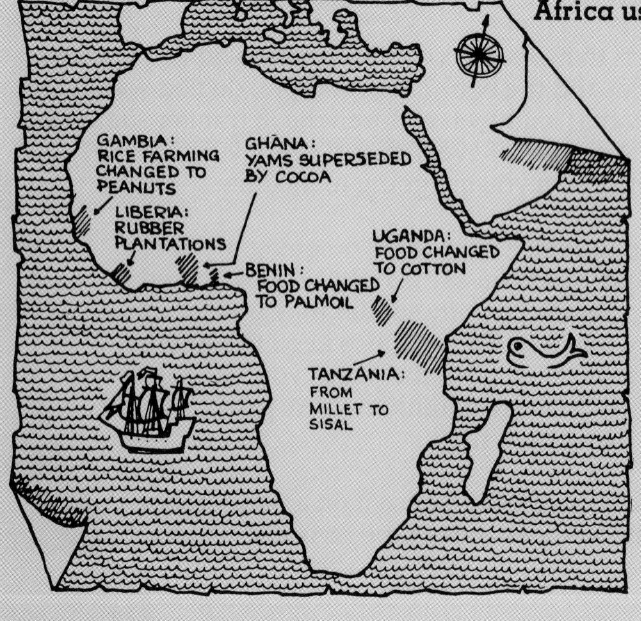

Much of the food produced in developing countries is grown for export, not for the ordinary people there to eat.

One company director forecas that Africa will become the world's largest producer of vegetables. Can Africans then look forward to the day when they will be well-fed? No; for most of the vegetables will be air-freighted out at great expense and served up at the tables of Europeans and Americans.

Some of the worst malnutritio in the world is to be found in Africa. Without the thousands of tons of imported grain most people wouldn't have enough eat. In the 1930s, however, Africa used to export grain.

In the last century or so, wherever Europeans settled or traded, they encouraged people to sow crops that we wanted in Europe. S cash crops (i.e. crop for sale) replaced food crops in many areas. Look what happened in Africa.

3 Food for animals

ore than a third of all the grain own in the world is used to ed animals. But in most untries meat is so expensive at the poor can rarely afford it.

In Colombia (South America) the traditional food crops are maize (sweetcorn) and certain types of beans. In the 1950s an American company started a chicken industry. Commercial farmers found they could make good profits by growing feed-crops for chickens, so less land was used to grow beans and maize which became more scarce and therefore more expensive. Did the poor people in Colombia start eating eggs and chicken? Unfortunately not, since a dozen eggs or two pounds of chicken cost more than an entire week's earnings for over a quarter of the population (1970 figures).

ereals and beans are the staple et of many people in the world. 'e in Britain eat a lot of haricot ans in the form of "baked ans".) But nowadays large antities of cereals, beans and h are fed to animals. As a sult, plenty of meat, milk, gs, etc., are produced, and e rich are able to eat much ore than is necessary for good alth.

Raising cattle or sheep may make good sense where land is unsuitable for growing crops. But when animals have to be fed large amounts of food which could be eaten by people, meat production is very wasteful.

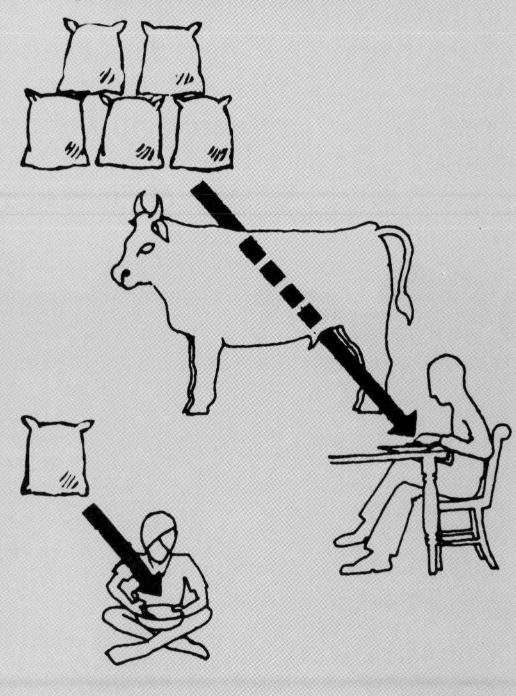

How much more grain does a person eating beef use up than a vegetarian?

n 1969/71 animals in the richer countries of the world ate more rain than all the people of India and China together – and no oubt they still do. How much better the poor might eat if this ood were available to them! How much cheaper cereals might e if people didn't have to compete with animals for them!

Vhy then, do so many people go hungry?

1. Why did farmers in Colombia start growing feedcrops for chickens?
2. Did the people of Colombia start eating meat? Did they have more or less to eat? Why?
3. What do you think happened to most of the chickens?
4. Look carefully at the diagram. What does it show about animals, people and grain?
5. Explain what the writer means when he/she says that 'people have to compete with animals'.

Tips for Success

- Don't try to put in everything you've read. Select the facts that you think you can explain to your audience and which will interest them.
- Order what you say carefully so that your audience can follow your arguments.
- Don't speak too fast. Look up as you talk. Speak loudly and clearly with as much expression as you can.
- Practise your talk several times before you give it.

ENOUGH FOR ALL

Eighteen children die of hunger, somewhere in the world, every minute of every day of the year. Some adults die as well, but most starvation deaths are among children.

There is enough food in the grain crops of Europe and North America to feed every child, woman and man on earth, and to keep them all fairly healthy. Even though we do not all want to live on grain, there is enough food around the world for everyone to have not only enough, but variety as well.

We know that not everyone does have enough. Why do children starve to death? * **Gandhi** said: 'There is enough for everyone's need, but not for everyone's greed.' People could take a bit more than they need, and there would still be enough. The real greed of a small part of the world's people spoils life for many.

The richest one-tenth of the people take just under half the world's resources, including food. The poorest half of the world's people get about a quarter of the resources between them.

The information on these pages is taken from a Save the Children book. Again, work in pairs or small groups, helping each other to understand the information and carry out the tasks.

1 Write down the three facts on these pages which you find most interesting.

2 Each paragraph makes an important point. Work out the point each paragraph is making and write it out in one sentence. The first paragraph is saying something like: 'Most of the people who die of hunger are children'.

Greed also spoils life by making people grow luxuries where they could be growing their own food. Poor people, and poor countries, need money for trade. So if rich people and rich countries say 'Grow flowers for us', 'Grow strawberries' – or tobacco, or other luxuries – land is taken up to earn money from cash crops that could be better used growing food for the local people. Trade is good and important, but this greed puts people into debt and then makes them hungry.

When accidents happen, people in different countries will help each other in times of trouble. There are big organizations to do this. The long-term need is to fight the forces that push the same poor people always to the bottom of the heap, however hard they work.

Children – all children – need food; there is enough.

△ This Chinese girl is enjoying a bowl of nutritious food. She has enough food and is quite sure there will be more tomorrow and every day.

◁ These children in Bangladesh are hungry. But now they know that food is coming, the worst fear has gone and they wait patiently.

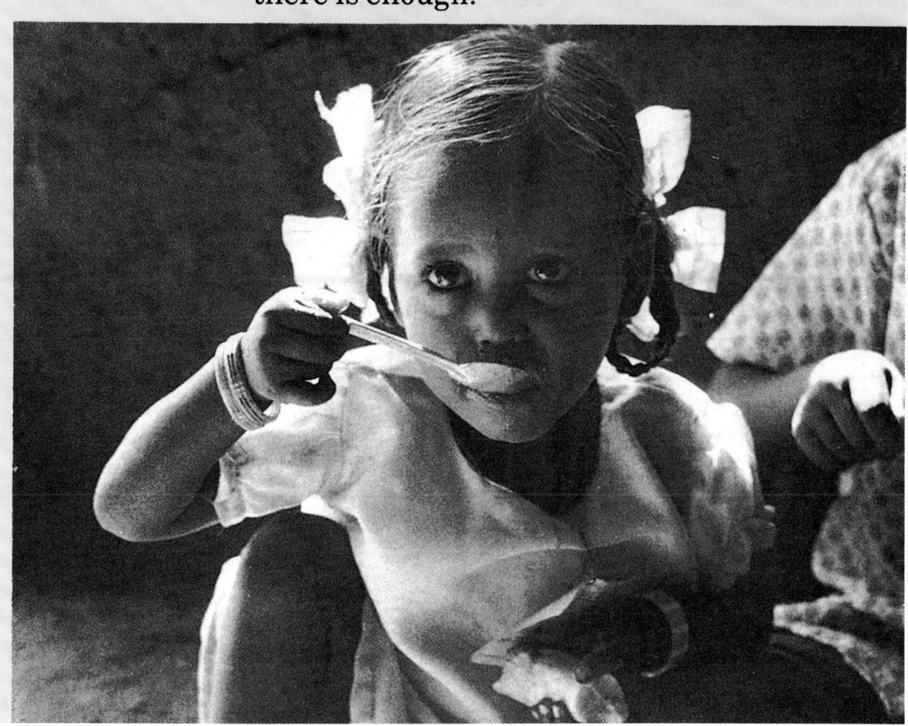

This South American girl ought to be sure of her food. But until the world's food is dealt with fairly, and the needs of children like her are met properly, there will always be worry in her eyes. ▷

Can your partner or group now answer the question: Why do so many go hungry?

Now go back to the first page of this unit and read how to prepare your short talk.

* Gandhi was an important Indian leader who lived earlier this century.

Acknowledgements

We would like to thank the following English teachers and advisers who have given advice, prepared units, trialled material in the classroom or commented on draft layouts for the Collins English Programme: Karen Alexander, Sandra Anstey, P. Baldwin, J. M. Barker, Phyllis Bell, Sue Bowles, Cathy Boyle, Graeme Burton, Robin Brabban, Glyn Bradbury, Mary de Caires, Peter Catmull, Mary Clark, Alan Combes, J. Coward, S. Crocker, Susan Daniels, J. Dawson, Reetha Desai, K. Downs, Kevin Eames, Philip Ellis, Alan Ellison, Dave Farrar, Angela Fitzgibbon, Jerry Fitzgibbon, Peter Foster, Gill Fox, Garrick Fraser, Mark Freeman, Janet Gaskell, Liz Gerschel, Dave Gilbert, Joan Goody, Arthur Graley, Sue Hart, I. Hathaway, Geoff Hill, A. and J. Hinchcliff, J. Hitchcock, David Horner, David Howe, Shelagh Hubbard, Mike Jones, Bridget Joslin, A. Khan-Cheema, E. Kircher, P. B. Knott, Stephen Kruger, D. Langford, Roger Lane, Margaret Leal, Patricia Lennon, M. J. Lunn, Sheila McCann, Norman Madden, John Mannion, D. Margett, Diti Mukherjee, Peter Murray, Mike Newman, Mark Ormiston, M. Parker, John Proctor, Jacqueline Purdie, P. Quirke, Stephen Richardson, Graham Robertson, Andy Roughton, Sean Russell, Patsy Spiller, P. Stock, John Sweetman, Enid Thirkell, C. Twist, Liz Vale, Mary Vass, Mike Vaughan Edwards, Ian Wall, Andrew Ward, A. Webb, Judi Webb, Ian Whitwam, John Williams, Richard Wilson, Stephen Wilson, S. Woodmansey.

Units for the Collins English Programme were trialled in the following schools: Blessed Edward Oldcorne, Worcester; Top Valley School, Nottingham; The Holy Cross School, Broadstairs; Bedwas Comprehensive School, Newport; St Michael's RC School, Watford; Myton School, Warwick; Williamwood High School, Glasgow; Wilcombe Middle School, Tiverton; Monkwearmouth School, Sunderland; King's High School, Warwick; The Hurst School, Baughurst; Salesian College, Farnborough; Thirsk School, Thirsk; The Aylesford School, Warwick; The Friary School, Lichfield; The Mountbatten School, Hemel Hempstead; Broomfield School, Havant; Claverham Community College, Battle; Chapter School, Rochester; Brockhill and St Leonards, Hythe; Stratford School, Newham; Camphill High School, Paisley; Ullapool High School, Ross and Cromarty; Pensby School for Girls, Wirral; Olchfa Comprehensive School, Swansea; Walton Comprehensive School, Peterborough; St Bede's High School, Blackburn; Oakfield School, Frome; Test Valley School, Stockbridge; Brookway High School, Wythenshawe; St Michael's School, Watford; Stratford High School, Stratford-upon-Avon; The National Comprehensive School, Hucknall; Wheeler's Lane School, Birmingham; Westhoughton High School, Westhoughton; Rugby High School for Girls, Rugby; Douay Martyrs Comprehensive School, Hillingdon.

The following authors and publishers are thanked for permission to reproduce their material: Edwin Morgan and Carcanet Press for *Off Course* and *The Computer's First Christmas Card*; Wes Magee and Unwin Hyman for *The Electric Household*; Jane Yolen and Macdonald & Co. for *The White Seal Maid* (from *Tales of Wonder*); Grace Hallworth and Methuen for *Never Play with Fire* (from *Mouth Open Story Jump Out*); Grace Nichols and Cambridge University Press for *Granny, Granny, Please Comb My Hair*; Vernon Scannell and Robson Books for *Dead Dog*; Leonard Clark and Hodder & Stoughton for *A Day in the Country*; Gareth Owen and Fontana for *Mog in the Dark*; John Burningham and Fontana for *Avocado Baby*; Eric Hill and Baker Books for *Where's Spot?*; Tony Ross and Fontana for *Towser and Sadie's Birthday*; Orchard Books and Bodley Head for their catalogues; Gerald Duckworth & Co. for *Jim* and *Matilda*; André Deutsch for *The Adventures of Isabel*; EMI Music Publishing Ltd and International Music Publications for *The Lion and Albert* (© 1933 Francis Day & Hunter Ltd); Oxfam, Save the Children. We would also like to thank Heinz, Marmite, Penguin (United Biscuits), Toshiba, Yop and the *Sun* for their help.

ILLUSTRATORS

David Eddington, Stuart Hughes, Amy Burch, Angie Sage, Sue Lines, Linda Garland, Simon Fell, Neil McDonald, Brian Sweet, M. L. Design, Hemesh Altes, Cathie Felsted, Anthony Kerins, Jane Bennett, Sharon Pallent, Robert Geary, Prue Berthon, Katy Bradbury, Shelley Jacobs, Karen Tushingham.

PHOTOGRAPHS

Russel Falkingham: pp. 14, 15, 83, 84, 85, 89; BBC Hulton Picture Library: pp. 8, 9 (except family group: Barnaby's Picture Library) and p. 111; Pictorial Press: p. 15 (Madonna); Keystone: p. 15 (Daley Thompson); Sally and Richard Greenhill: p. 36; Camerapix: p. 123; The Hutchinson Library: p. 125 (top).

THE DIAMOND GAME STATEMENTS

1. the way the beginning lets you know straightaway it's going to be a ghost story.
2. the way Justin gradually finds out about everything.
3. the way the bicycles seem almost like characters in the story.
4. the way Henry seems to be such a mysterious person.
5. the way the story mixes the past and the present.
6. the way the phantom cyclist keeps appearing and disappearing, so we are almost certain she is a ghost before Justin knows it.
7. the way the phantom cyclist seems to be a mixture of good and bad.
8. the way the story starts slowly and then builds up to an exciting climax on the cliff.
9. the way you don't know exactly how Uncle Henry and the phantom cyclist are linked until quite near the end.